Hotel Law
A Concise Guide to the
Law of Inns and Innkeepers

David Grant

Helen Douglas

Julia Sharpley

NORTHUMBRIA
LAW • PRESS

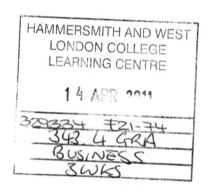

Published in 2007 by Northumbria Law Press,
Northumbria University, Newcastle upon Tyne NE1 8ST

© Northumbria University 2007

ISBN 978 0 9553286 5 7

Designed and produced by Northumbria University,
Newcastle upon Tyne NE1 8ST.

186395B/H/B/02/07

PREFACE

The best of modern hotels are seductive institutions with their enormous glass and chrome atriums, their spas and health clubs, their attentive service, their plush public spaces, their equally luxurious rooms and their fine dining. Names like the Ritz, the Savoy and Claridges are by words for luxury and opulence. But not all hotels reach such standards and many of us will have experienced hotels that could compete on even terms with Fawlty Towers – the surly service, indifferent food, dirty rooms, grimy baths, dark corridors, lumpy beds, and even, on occasion, bed bugs. Historically of course things were even worse. Not only did travellers have to tolerate poor conditions they were also prey to thieves and robbers – often in league with the innkeepers themselves. It was in circumstances such as this that the early law of inns and innkeeping developed – imposing stringent conditions on innkeepers for the protection of the traveller and his property. And it is for this reason that much of the law on hotels seems slightly dated, even quaint. The concept that a traveller has a legal right to be accommodated does not sit well with modern views on freedom of contract and freedom of choice. Likewise the hotelkeeper's strict liability for his guest's goods and the corresponding right of lien over them as security for payment are not particularly familiar legal principles. Nevertheless these concepts are part of the modern law of hotelkeeping – which is all the more interesting for them.

In this book we have endeavoured to state the law which regulates the relationship between the hotelkeeper and his guests as it is today. We do so by drawing upon the rich legacy of English case law which we have supplemented where appropriate with materials from other common law jurisdictions and Scotland. It is our intention that it will not only serve as a text book and a source of valuable materials to lawyers but it will also be accessible to a wider audience of lay readers who have an interest in hotel law and management.

David Grant
Fairfax, Virginia, August 2006.

Contents

TABLE OF CASES

TABLE OF LEGISLATION

Foreign Legislation

European Legislation

REPORTS

CHAPTER ONE
THE DEFINITION OF AN HOTEL
FAWLTY TOWERS OR BATES MOTEL?

General Introduction

The law of inns and innkeepers in England and Wales, by which we mean the legal relationship which exists between an innkeeper and his guests, is a much ignored branch of English law. Apart from brief sections in general books on hospitality law[1] and a section in Halsbury's Law of England, there is virtually no modern literature or caselaw on the subject. It is possible to speculate on the reasons for this: perhaps it is because the principles are so well settled that litigation is unnecessary; perhaps it is because, like other areas of travel law, the sums involved are so small and consumers so unwilling to pursue their claims that disputes do not reach the courts. It may just be that the name of this branch of the law, the law of inns and innkeepers, is simply so unappealing and old-fashioned that commentators are not attracted by it.

Whatever the reasons it is hard to believe that a service industry which generates over £11 billion pounds of business per annum in the UK[2] is entirely free from conflict and therefore unworthy of comment. Certainly this is not the case across the Atlantic where lawyers are served by several major works which devote considerable comment to the accommodation sector of the travel industry.[3]

---

1   See for instance 'Hospitality and Tourism Law', Poustie et al, 1999; 'Principles of Hospitality Law', Boella and Pannett, 2nd ed., 1999.

2   In 2006 it is estimated that the hotel industry will generate £11.2 billion in revenue. Source: Mintel: Hotels – UK – 2006.

3   John EH Sherry, The Laws of Innkeeper, 3rd ed. 1993; Robert M Jarvis et al, Travel Law: Cases and Materials, 1998; TA Dickerson, Travel Law 1981–2006

We hope therefore in this book to be able to redress the balance as far as English law is concerned by examining some of the key concepts in this area of the law. We start by examining what is meant by an 'inn'. However before we do so, a word on terminology. For centuries, the accepted terminology for what we would now consider to be 'hotels' and 'hoteliers' has been 'inns' and 'innkeepers'. Now that we are well into the new millennium it seems appropriate to adopt a more modern terminology. Most tourists would be puzzled to discover that the bright, modern, city-centre, glass and concrete 'hotel' into which they have booked is in fact correctly called an 'inn' – a term which conjures up 'olde England', flagons of warm beer and stagecoaches. We have therefore decided to use the terms 'hotel' and 'hotelkeeper', 'hotelier' or 'hotel proprietor' whenever possible. We accept that there will be instances where this usage is not technically correct for there are occasions when what may be called an hotel is not an inn, but where this is so we will indicate accordingly, and, where the context demands it we shall retain the old terminology.

Given the paucity of materials on hotel law we have also adopted a policy, space permitting, of quoting at length from source materials in the body of the text rather than relegating the substance of what we want to say to footnotes. We hope that this not only provides a useful body of source materials but also helps to convey some of the richness of this neglected area of the law.

What is an hotel?

The origins of hotel law go back to medieval times and much of it is based upon the custom of the realm. An hotelkeeper was regarded as belonging to one of the 'common callings' and as such was subject to particular rights and liabilities: the obligation to receive guests; strict liability for the property of guests; and a right of lien over guests' property. These rights and duties still exist today and depend upon it being possible to say that the hotelkeeper is running an 'hotel'.

The starting point of our examination of the meaning of this term is the Hotel Proprietors Act 1956 (HPA).[4] This Act was passed following the Law Reform Committee's Second Report: 'Innkeepers' Liability for Property of Travellers, Guests and Residents'.[5] The Report was published following a referral to the Committee by the Lord Chancellor of the question of 'whether any changes are desirable in the law relating to innkeepers' liability in respect of the property of travellers, guests and residents'. What appears to have prompted the commissioning of the Report was the decision in *Williams v Linnitt*[6] which turned on the meaning of 'traveller' and the extent to which an hotelkeeper was liable for the traveller's property. We will be looking at this issue in a later chapter but in the meantime the relevance of the Report to the present discussion is that one of the Committee's recommendations was that:

> "It is desirable that any new legislation should contain a definition of an inn based on the existing common law meaning of the term."[7]

With a speed which now appears remarkable Parliament took up the recommendations of the Committee and passed the HPA in 1956. In section one we find the following definition of hotel:

> "S.1(3) In this Act, the expression "hotel" means an establishment held out by the proprietor as offering food, drink and, if so required, sleeping accommodation, without special contract, to any traveller presenting himself who appears able and willing to pay a reasonable sum for the services and facilities provided and who is in a fit state to be received."

The origins of this definition of an hotel can be clearly traced back to the existing common law definition of an inn. For instance in

---

4   *See Appendix One*
5   *May 1954, Cmd. 9161*
6   *[1951] 1 KB 565*
7   *Para. 16(8) p.8*

Thompson v Lacy[8] Bayley J said:

> "I think, therefore, that in point of law this is an inn, and that the defendant is under the obligations to which innkeepers are liable, viz, that he is bound to receive all persons who are capable of paying a reasonable compensation for the accommodation provided, and that he is liable for their goods, if lost or stolen; and, on the other hand, that he has a lien on the goods of his guests for the payment of his bill."

Later in the same case Best J gave this definition of an inn:

> "An inn is a house, the owner of which holds out that he will receive all travellers and sojourners who are willing to pay a price adequate to the sort of accommodation provided, and who come in a situation in which they are fit to be received."

These statements were widely accepted at common law as the definition of inn[9] and it is evident that the statutory definition is no more than a restatement of the common law.

Looking at the definition more closely it can be broken down into a number of elements. If an establishment is to be regarded as an hotel it has to be shown that:

● the establishment is held out

● as offering food, drink and, if so required, sleeping accommodation

● without special contract

● to any traveller

● who appears able and willing to pay a reasonable sum

● and who is in a fit state to be received

---

8 *(1820) 3 B & Ald 283; 106 ER 667*

9 *Cunningham v Philp (1896) 12 TLR 352 and Orchard v Bush [1898] 2QB 284*

Looking at it another way an hotelkeeper runs an establishment where he holds himself out as providing all the basic needs of a traveller and is under an obligation to receive any traveller who turns up at his door who is in a fit state and able to pay. The essence of the definition is that the traveller has a *right* to be accommodated in an establishment which is *held out* as providing for all his basic needs.

It is with the first three elements of this definition that we are concerned in this chapter. The other elements will be dealt with in subsequent chapters as they are not so much concerned with what an hotel is, so much as who the hotelkeeper must receive and on *what terms*.

Holding out

To be an hotel an establishment must be shown to have been held out as willing to accept any traveller without special contract. This is a question of fact on which the definition offers no help. This was remarked upon at the time of the passage of the Act:

> "....in framing the definition of an hotel (s.1(3)), Parliament has taken so literally the committee's recommendations that such a definition should be based on their existing common-law meaning of the term 'inn' as to leave precisely as before the question whether any particular house is or is not an inn, or an hotel ... The criterion is this: Did the proprietor hold out the establishment as offering food, drink and, if so required, sleeping accommodation, without special contract, to any traveller presenting himself who appeared able and willing to pay a reasonable sum for the services and facilities provided and who was in a fit state to be received? How is the proper answer to this question to be forecast by the traveller when he first comes to the threshold of the hostelry? That is the stage at which the exact legal position ought to be ascertainable by him. No doubt most inns and hotels which fulfil this description do so to notoriety. But

as to the rest, an individual traveller only knows what sort of reception he had when he made it known that he wanted a bed or a meal."[10]

The solution proposed by the author of the article was to inaugurate a system of 'indelible labelling':

"If persons who desired or were willing to conduct hotels as described in the Act were given an absolute monopoly of the word "hotel," and required to exhibit it in a prominent place *outside* the premises, or were subjected to compulsory registration, we should all know better where we were."

This eminently sensible solution has not been adopted so we are left only with what guidance we can derive from the caselaw. The case is different in other jurisdictions such as Ireland for instance where a statutory registration scheme has been adopted.[11]

A sign might be one indication of whether an establishment was an hotel or not but in the words of Holt CJ in *Parker v Flint*[12]:

"... a sign is not essential to an inn, but is an evidence of it."

Also on the question of signs, in Halsbury's Law of England[13] there is a note to the effect that:

"To pull down a sign appears to be evidence that the house is no longer an inn, but if after pulling down the sign the house is still used for receiving and entertaining travellers it is just as much an inn as if it had a sign: *Anon* (1623) 2 Roll Rep 345"

It might be thought that what an establishment chooses to call itself

---

10 'Innkeepers' Liability', J.F.J., (1937) 101 Sol. Jo. 137
11 See 'Hotel, Restaurant & Public House Law', Marc McDonald, Dublin, 1992
12 (1699) 12 Mod Rep 254
13 Vol. 24, Para 1101

would be an indication of its status but with hotels this is not so. In *Thompson v Lacy* Bayley CJ said of the 'Globe Tavern and Coffee House' (which the court decided was an inn) that:

> "In order to learn its character, we must look to the use to which it is applied, and not merely to the name by which it is designated."

You only have to open the Yellow Pages at the section on 'Hotels and Inns' to see the confusion that exists. In this section of our own local pages there are a variety of names for hotels, including not only 'Inn' and 'Hotel' but also 'Lodge' and 'Arms' and 'House' but these names are not an accurate reflection of what they are, for it is possible to identify establishments that are clearly not hotels – including a number of 'bed and breakfast' establishments and also a university college offering accommodation to the public. Turning to the section on 'Public Houses' the same confusion can be found. The list is littered with 'Inns' and 'Hotels' which are no such thing – merely bars masquerading as something more substantial.

The Law Reform Committee, whilst acknowledging that, '... one of the unsatisfactory features of the present law is the difficulty of ascertaining whether the premises in question constitute an inn or not' nevertheless had this to say on resolving the problem:

> "... we think that the difficulty of deciding whether or not any given establishment is an inn is probably greater in theory than in practice, for it seems likely that the owner of any premises whose status might be doubtful will have concluded the question against himself by exhibiting the statutory notice under the Act of 1863." [A predecessor to the 1956 Act]

A similar point is made by Sherry[14]:

> "In determining the question, [whether an establishment is an inn or a private house] the facts may lead to a

---

14   *At p.11*

---

presumption against a party. Thus if a housekeeper does an act which he could not legally do unless he were an innkeeper, he will be presumed, in the absence of evidence to the contrary, to be an innkeeper. Thus in *Korn v Schedler*, 11 Daly (NY) 234 (Ct CPNY Co. 1882) it was held that when a man has applied for a license to sell liquor as a hotelkeeper, he cannot later deny liability for the loss of a guest's property on the ground that he does not keep a hotel."

However at least one commentator[15] is not convinced by this:

"Not even the display of the statutory notice is a foolproof guide, since the notice itself contains a clause stating that the mere display of the notice cannot be regarded as evidence that the establishment is an inn."

The relevant part of the 1956 Act is found in the Schedule and reads as follows:

"This notice does not constitute an admission either that the Act applies to this hotel or that liability thereunder attaches to the proprietor of this hotel in any particular case."

There is some strength in Field's view. As pointed out by Blom-Cooper,[16] in the case of *Olley v Marlborough Court Ltd*[17] such a notice was displayed by what the court called a 'private residential hotel' but the court was happy to accept that it was not an hotel at common law.

It might be thought that the keeping of a register is an indication that the proprietor is running an hotel but unfortunately this is not the case. The Immigration (Hotel Records) Order 1972[18] which requires proprietors to keep a register applies to:

---

15 David Field, 'Hotel and Catering Law, 5th ed. 1988, p.185
16 LJ Blom-Cooper, 'Reports of Committees', (1955) 18 MLR 374
17 [1949] 1 KB 582
18 SI 1972 No 1689

"... any hotel or other premises, whether furnished or unfurnished, where lodging or sleeping accommodation is provided for reward." (Reg. 3)

Field suggests[19] that one way to approach the issue of holding out is to look for indications to the contrary, so for instance he suggests that an hotel that had a sign up saying 'no coaches' or 'no children' or 'booking by prior contract only' would not be hotels because they clearly held themselves out as *not* being prepared to accept all travellers.

Another approach, given the scarcity of English caselaw, would be to look at other jurisdictions which have adopted English law or are based on the common law. Here we are fortunate, for in the US we find a number of cases, all cited in Sherry, where this issue has been explored. In *State v Stone*[20] the court said that an inn was an establishment kept:

"... publicly, openly and notoriously, for the entertainment and accommodation of travellers and others, for a reward."

In *Lyon v Smith*[21] Chief Justice Mason said:

"To render a person liable as a common innkeeper, it is not sufficient to show that he occasionally entertains travellers. Most of the farmers in a new country do this, without supposing themselves answerable for the horses or other property of their guests, which may be stolen, or otherwise lost, without any fault of their own. Nor is such the rule in older countries, where it would operate with far less injustice, and be less opposed to good policy than with us. To be subjected to the same responsibilities attaching to innkeepers, a person must make tavern-keeping, to some extent, a regular business, a means of livelihood. He should hold himself out to the world as an innkeeper.

---

19   *p.185*

20   *6 Vt. 295 (1834)*

21   *1 Iowa 244 (1843)*

It is not necessary that he should have a sign, or a license, provided that he has in any other manner authorised the general understanding that his was a public house, where strangers had a right to require accommodation. The person who occasionally entertains others for a reasonable compensation is no more subject to the extraordinary responsibility of an innkeeper than is he liable as a common carrier, who in certain special cases carries the property of others from one place to another for hire."

As Sherry admits however:

"The question whether a house where a guest is entertained is a public inn or a private house is a question of fact, to be determined, like any fact, upon all the evidence."[22]

Thus the question of whether an establishment is held out as an hotel, short of the kind of statutory intervention discussed above, will continue to cause difficulties in marginal cases, compounded by the fact that as Field observes:

"... there appears to be nothing to prevent a proprietor changing from an inn to a private hotel, or vice versa, whenever he wishes."[23]

Offering food, drink and, if so required, sleeping accommodation

An hotel must cater for all the traveller's basic needs so an establishment which does not do so cannot be an hotel. Here the caselaw is more helpful. For instance in *R v Rymer*[24] it was held that a bar which was under the same roof as an hotel but entirely separate from it, with a separate entrance was not an hotel and therefore the proprietor was not under an obligation to receive the prosecutor.

---

22 *p.11*
23 *p.185*
24 *(1877) 2 QBD 136*

Two cases, *Pidgeon v Legge*[25] and *Sealey v Tandy*,[26] both involving the ejection of disorderly guests, contain observations that a mere alehouse or public house is not an inn. Similarly a restaurant alone is not an inn[27] but note that where the restaurant is part of the hotel then the obligations of the hotelkeeper extend to guests who are merely eating in the restaurant.[28]

Lodging houses, boarding houses and residential hotels are not hotels. Although these establishments all offer accommodation they are not hotels for a number of reasons: First, because they do not hold themselves out as being prepared to receive all comers (see above); secondly because they do not entertain 'travellers' (to be dealt with in a subsequent chapter); thirdly because the legal basis of their transactions is contract rather than the custom of the realm; and fourthly, a reason related to the third, but of particular relevance here, many of them do not offer food and if they do, it is on the basis of *contract*. In *Dansey v Richardson*[29] for instance the defendant entertained the plaintiff at her boarding house where the plaintiff was provided with the 'use and occupation of rooms ... and with meat, drink and servant's attendance'. Despite being provided with precisely the same kind of services that would have been available at an hotel this was nevertheless a boarding house – designed for guests who stayed for long periods and who *contracted* for the services on a weekly basis.

Dansey v Richardson is a relatively straightforward case but at the margins however it may be difficult to distinguish lodging houses and boarding houses from hotels. For example in *Parker v Flint*[30] it was held that the establishment in question was only a lodging house because the proprietor was not compelled to entertain everybody and

---

25   *(1857) 21 JP 743*

26   *[1902] 1 KB 296*

27   *Ultzen v Nichols [1894] 1 QB 92*

28   *Orchard v Bush [1898] 2 QB 284*

29   *(1854) 118 ER 1095, 1311*

30   *(1699) 12 Mod Rep 254*

'none could come there without previous contract'. However Holt CJ went on to remark:

> " ... that if one comes to an inn, and make a previous contract for lodging for a set time, and do not eat or drink there, he is no guest , but a lodger, and as such is not under the innkeeper's protection; but if he eat and drink there it is otherwise; or if he pay for his diet there, though he do not take it there."

Modern forms of accommodation such as bed and breakfast establishments (B&B's) and motels will not be hotels either. The reason for this is that although they may provide food as well as accommodation the service they supply in this respect is only limited. Thus they are not catering for all the traveller's needs. By their very nature B&B's generally only offer breakfast and even where they offer an evening meal this is not because the traveller has a *right* to it because it is an inn, rather it is a service which can be contracted for. Motels may offer more or less than a B&B in terms of food but in that they do not hold themselves out as offering a full meal service to travellers they too are not hotels.

On the question of drink it has been held that this does not necessarily mean alcoholic drink. In *Cunningham v Philp*[31] it was held that a temperance hotel was nevertheless an hotel. Cave J said that he could hardly see how temperance principles could turn an hotel into a boarding house.

The fact that a traveller is lawfully refused a meal at an establishment, even when he is fit to be received, does not necessarily mean however that it is not an hotel. In *R v Higgins*[32] a traveller was refused food even though others who had booked tables in advance were being served. In quashing the verdict of the jury in the lower court Lord Goddard CJ said that a hotel proprietor was entitled to refuse to serve a guest if he had reasonable grounds for doing so. It was suggested that in a time of

---

31 *(1896) 12 TLR 352*
32 *[1948] 1 KB 165*

---

rationing it was reasonable to reserve what food the proprietor had for guests who had already booked. Similarly, in *Browne v Brandt*,[33] an hotelkeeper was within his rights to refuse to accommodate a traveller when there were no rooms available in the hotel.

Without Special Contract

A traveller who turns up unannounced at an hotel, without prior agreement or notice has a *right* to be accommodated by the hotel. This is the essence of an hotel – that it will receive travellers who simply arrive on the doorstep needing refreshment or a bed for the night. They cannot be turned away into the night, prey to robbers and bandits. The case of *R v Ivens*[34] illustrates the point admirably:

"The facts in this case do not appear to be much in dispute; and though I do not recollect to have ever heard of such an indictment having been tried before, the law applicable to this case is this:– that an indictment lies against an innkeeper, who refuses to receive a guest, he having at the time room in his house; and either the price of the guest's entertainment being tendered to him, or such circumstances occurring as will dispense with that tender. This law is founded in good sense. The innkeeper is not to select his guests. He has no right to say to one, you shall come into my inn, and to another you shall not, as every one coming and conducting himself in a proper manner has a right to be received and for this purpose innkeepers are a sort of public servants, they having in return a kind of privilege of entertaining travellers, and supplying them with what they want. It is said in the present case, that Mr. Williams, the prosecutor, conducted himself improperly, and therefore ought not to have been admitted into the house of the defendant. If a person came to an inn drunk, or behaved in an indecent or improper manner, I am of

---

33   *[1902] 1 KB 696*
34   *173 ER 94*

opinion that the innkeeper is not bound to receive him. You will consider whether Mr. Williams did so behave here. It is next said that he came to the inn at a late hour of the night, when probably the family were gone to bed. Have we not all knocked at inn doors at late hours of the night, and after the family have retired to rest, not for the purpose of annoyance, but to get the people up? In this case it further appears, that the wife of the defendant has a conversation with the prosecutor, in which she insists on knowing his name and abode. I think that an innkeeper has no right to insist on knowing those particulars; and certainly you and I would think an innkeeper very impertinent, who asked either the one or the other of any of us. However, the prosecutor gives his name and residence; and supposing that he did add the words "and be damned to you," is that a sufficient reason for keeping a man out of an inn who has travelled till midnight? I think that the prosecutor was not guilty of such misconduct as would entitle the defendant to shut him out of his house. It has been strongly objected against the prosecutor by Mr. Godson, that he had been travelling on a Sunday. To make that argument of any avail, it must be contended that travelling on a Sunday is illegal. It is not so, although it is what ought to be avoided whenever it can be. Indeed there is one thing which shews that travelling on a Sunday is not illegal, which is, that in many places you pay additional toll at the turnpikes if you pass through them on a Sunday, by which the legislature plainly contemplates travelling on a Sunday as a thing not illegal. I do not encourage travelling on Sundays, but still it is not illegal. With respect to the non-tender of money by the prosecutor, it is now a custom so universal with innkeepers to trust that a person will pay before he leaves an inn, that it cannot be necessary for a guest to tender money before he goes into an inn; indeed, in the present case, no objection was made that Mr. Williams did not make a tender; and they did not even insinuate that they had any suspicion that he could not pay for whatever entertainment might be furnished to him. I think, therefore, that that cannot be set up as a defence. It however remains for me next to consider the case with respect to the hour of the night at which Mr. Williams applied for admission; and the opinion which I have formed is, that the lateness of the hour is no excuse to the defendant for refusing to receive the prosecutor into his inn. Why are inns established? For the reception of travellers, who are often very far distant from their own homes. Now, at what time is it most essential that travellers should not be denied admission into the inns? I should say when they are benighted, and when, from any casualty, or from the badness of the roads, they arrive at an inn at a very late hour. Indeed, in former times, when the roads were much worse, and were much infested with robbers, a late hour of the night was the time, of all others, at which the traveller most required to be received into an inn. I think, therefore, that if the traveller conducts himself properly, the innkeeper is bound to admit him, at whatever hour of the night he may arrive. The only other question in this case is, whether the defendants' inn was full. There is no distinct evidence on the part of the prosecution that it was not. But I think the conduct of the parties shews that the inn was not full; because, if it had been, there could have been no use in the landlady asking the prosecutor his name, and saying, that if he would tell it, she would ring for one of the servants." (Coleridge J).

But what of the traveller who has made prior arrangements, as most people do nowadays? If an establishment does receive such a guest, who has *contracted* to stay, in what capacity is he received – as an hotel guest, or as a lodger or a boarder? Here the issue is not so much whether the establishment is an hotel or not, rather what is the status of the person staying at the establishment? This question will be dealt with in Chapter Two. However for the present it is sufficient to reiterate what was said above, that an establishment that takes only guests by virtue of contract and does not hold itself out as being prepared to accept all comers is not an hotel.

The hospitium of the hotel

One further question needs to be answered before we leave the definition of an hotel. What is meant by the *hospitium* of the hotel and how far does it extend? The importance of this derives from the fact that the hotelkeeper is strictly liable for a guest's property which is *infra hospitium* but not otherwise. The problem arose fairly and squarely in the case of *Williams v Linnitt*[35] in which the plaintiff had had his car stolen from the car park of the Royal Red Gate Inn near Nuneaton. As well as the issue of whether the plaintiff was a 'traveller' it had to be decided whether the car park came within the hospitium of the hotel. It is evident from the following extract that the hospitium of the hotel is not co-extensive with the boundaries of the property of the hotel; it is a more confined area, limited to the curtilage of the hotel or to areas where the hotelkeeper has extended the *hospitium* beyond the curtilage by accepting responsibility for the guests property in that area.

> "The second defence raised was that the car park was not within "the *hospitium*" of the inn. The car park consists of a wide triangular space in front of the inn which opens on to it, with the road from Watling Street to Fenny Drayton running along the side of the inn. The car park has a tar macadam surface and there is a large sign with the words "Royal Red Gate" in conspicuous letters across one side of the park. It was clearly constructed and intended for the parking of visitors' cars and was so used. There was, however, attached to one of the uprights supporting the sign a small square board with the following notice on it:

---

35 *[1951] 1 KB 565*

'Car Park. Patrons only. Vehicles are admitted to this parking place on condition that the proprietor shall not be liable for loss of or damage to (a) any vehicle (b) anything in or on or about any vehicle, however, such loss or damage may be caused. R. W. Linnitt. Proprietor.'

The learned judge found that the plaintiff had not seen, or, at any rate, read, the notice and that, in any event, if the car park was part of the inn, such a notice would not relieve the innkeeper of his common law liability. The defendant, on appeal, did not seek to rely on this notice as contractually relieving him from liability, and conceded that, if the car park was within the *"hospitium,"* he could not contract out of his liability, but he contended that the *"hospitium"* of an inn *prima facie* includes only the inn itself, its stables, and (in modern times) its garages, though it may be extended beyond the stables or garages by the innkeeper either by accepting the goods by himself or his servants or by necessary inference from his conduct: see *Jones v Tyler*.[36] This extension being within the control of the innkeeper, he can, it is said, exclude by notice the extension which might otherwise have been inferred from the circumstances. There is no doubt that in former times the *"hospitium"* was limited to the inn and stables and that the innkeeper was not liable for his guest's horse which was put to pasture by the guest in a field adjoining the inn, but there is no authority which limits the *"hospitium"* to such parts of the premises as are under cover, and the word *"infra"* has been treated as equivalent to *"intra"*. It is conceded that in modern times the *"hospitium"* extends to garages, and I can see no reason why it should not include car parks designed and intended for the use of customers paying visits of short duration, just as in former times the gig would be left in the yard on market days. This applies particularly in cases like the present where the inn, adjoining Watling Street, is obviously catering for motor traffic and where no evidence was given by the defendant as to the existence or extent or situation of any garages in which visitors might place their cars. It is true that in the course of the trial a plan, other than the plan which had been agreed, was received in evidence, and that plan does indicate the existence of such garages at the top of the plan. No evidence was given to explain the situation or nature of these garages or whether they belonged to the defendant or some other person. Therefore, I proceed on the basis that there was, in fact, no evidence of the existence of any garages attached to or forming part of the inn.

The liability of the innkeeper, in my view, extends to the goods of his guest which are placed by the guest in that part of the premises in which such goods are usually taken in the inn. The innkeeper will not be responsible if a motor car is placed by the guest on some part of the inn premises not intended for, and unsuitable for, the reception of motor vehicles. This is, I think, the explanation of the old cases, such as *Harland's Case*,[37] *Brand v Glasse*[38] and *Sanders v Spencer*,[39] where a distinction is drawn between an "outyard" and an "inner yard." If an innkeeper has an "inner yard" more suitable for the reception of carriages or cars, he can no doubt exclude the user for this purpose of an "outer yard," but, if he has only one yard or car parking space forming part of the inn premises and designed and intended for the use of cars and if he offers no other accommodation for his customers' cars, then I can see no reason why such space is not within the "*hospitium*".

37 *(1641), Clay 97*
38 *72 ER 503*
39 *73 ER 591*

Furthermore, if liability is to be determined by the structural nature of the yard, I would ask what are the determining features? Must there be a wall or building on all sides of the space or will a wall on two sides or three sides suffice? Suppose the inn building forms one side of the yard, but on two other sides it is bordered by the walls of adjoining buildings with a gateway or archway leading into the street. Is this an inner yard? Unless I can find some guidance from the authorities as to the answer to such questions as these I prefer what seems to be a more reasonable test, namely, is the place in question a part of the inn premises intended and suitable for user in connection with some part of the innkeeper's business, and, if I find that it is not only intended and suitable for such purpose, but is the only accommodation available for the particular purpose, then it seems to me that such part of the premises must necessarily be within the *"hospitium"* of the inn. If an innkeeper holds himself out as willing to receive customers' motor cars on his premises, he is responsible for their safety. In the present case the defendant so held himself out, there was no evidence of any other accommodation for motor cars, and, in my opinion, the *"hospitium"* of this inn included the car park and the defendant cannot escape liability for the safety of his guests' motor cars parked in the place intended for them merely by exhibiting a notice such as that described above.

One further matter remains to be dealt with. It was said that one of the plans put in evidence at the trial showed that the only access to the saloon bar visited by the plaintiff was from the outside and consequently it did not form part of the premises devoted to the business of an innkeeper. Further inspection of the plan showed that there was apparently access to this bar from the rear, through a courtyard on to which other parts of the premises opened.

No evidence was given on this matter at the trial and the
learned judge did not deal with it in his judgment. The
material available is manifestly insufficient to enable us to
say that this well known feature of most inns was not an
integral part of the inn premises. For these reasons, I think
this appeal fails." (Lord Tucker)

Denning LJ gave a dissenting judgment on the grounds that the
hotelkeeper was permitted to exclude his liability but his observations
on what constituted the *hospitium* of the inn were very much in line
with those of Lord Tucker.

CHAPTER TWO
WHO IS A TRAVELLER?
FROM PACK HORSE TO PACKAGE HOLIDAYS

Introduction

The first chapter examined what, in legal terms, an hotel is. In this chapter we turn our attention towards whom the hotelkeeper must receive. In other words, we address the question: who is a 'traveller' or a 'guest'?

Historically, it was a matter of considerable public interest that any traveller (with some exceptions) be received at an inn or hotel as of right. That is, in an era when travelling was difficult and dangerous, the common law evolved to ensure that the travelling public did not have to depend upon the whim or caprice of the individual hotelier in providing them with food and shelter. Running an inn was a 'common or public calling', hence an innkeeper was not free to contract with particular individuals but rather they were duty bound to serve all travellers that applied. This was accepted practice as early as the fifteenth century; in 1460, Moile J. is quoted:

> "... if I come to an innkeeper to lodge with him, and he will not lodge me, I shall have on my case an action of trespass against him ..."[40]

Moreover, owing to the proliferation of untrustworthy innkeepers in ancient times, the law also developed to protect the belongings of a traveller staying as a guest at an inn or hotel by making the innkeeper strictly liable for a traveller's possessions that were within the hospitium of the hotel. *Calye's Case*,[41] decided in 1584, is one of the

---

40   *Y.B. 39 H. VI. 18.24. cited in 17 Harvard Law Review 156 (1903)*
41   *(1584) 8 Co. Rep. 32a; 77 ER 520*

oldest and most often quoted authorities on this point. Grose J. considers the effect of *Calye* in the later case of *Bennett v Mellor*:[42]

> "According to that, if a man go into an inn and is accepted there as a guest, the innkeeper is bound to take care of the goods of the guest..."

Of course, travel today is entirely different. For example many people, particularly in Europe and, to a lesser extent in the US, would not consider turning up at an hotel unannounced without first checking for vacancies or making a booking. Similarly, few would consider themselves or their belongings to be at great risk on a domestic journey. Nevertheless, the age-old concept that hotels exist to serve the needy wayfarer or traveller who turns up unannounced, and to protect their belongings during their stay, still remains the basis of hotel law both in England and in other countries. Therefore an understanding of 'who is a traveller?' is fundamental to the understanding of hotel law.

Who is a traveller?

In one sense, the traveller can be defined according to the rights and obligations attached to him. A traveller was, and still is, a special class of person to whom the hotelier owes two primary obligations: the duty to receive him and, where he is accepted as a guest at an hotel, the duty to take care of his property. The traveller therefore has a right of criminal and civil action against the hotelier who refuses to receive him without reasonable excuse. He also has a civil right of action to recover from the proprietor the value of property stolen during his stay as a guest at an hotel. The corollary to these stringent obligations is that the hotelier has a right of lien on the belongings that a traveller brings into the inn.

However, this still doesn't tell us who a traveller is. It is important to understand who belongs to this special class as it is only travellers who are entitled to enforce these special obligations resting on an hotelier.[43]

---

42 *5 Term 276*

43 *R v Luellin 88 ER 1441; 12 Mod 446 for indictment and Grimston v Innkeeper (1627) Het 49; 124 ER 334 for civil action.*

This is not as straightforward as it may sound.

There is no set definition of a traveller, statutory or otherwise. Instead, an understanding of the word has evolved and been modified over centuries of caselaw decisions. Moreover, there are two strands of caselaw concerned with the definition of 'traveller': those cases that relate to a traveller's right to be received; and the larger body of caselaw that relates to the hotelier's duty to protect a traveller's belongings once a traveller has been received as a guest. In the latter strand of caselaw there is also potential for some confusion when attempting to define a 'traveller', because legal terminology dictates that once a traveller has been received at an hotel he is referred to as a 'guest'. Often, in the cases, only the word guest is used and the word traveller is not mentioned. Therefore, before we go on to look in more detail at the development of the caselaw and subsequently the Hotel Proprietors Act 1956, it is worth examining the relationship between 'guest' and 'traveller' more closely.

Travellers, guests and the innkeeper/guest relationship

Understanding the relationship between 'guest' and 'traveller' is particularly important in the context of claims made against hoteliers for liability for stolen belongings. This is because, to succeed, a claimant must be able to show that he has *become* a guest at an hotel and that, consequently, an innkeeper/guest relationship has arisen between himself and the hotelier. Where this is the case, the innkeeper becomes liable as insurer of the claimant's goods. Whether this relationship has been established is a question of fact for the courts to decide. However, one factor in determining the existence of such a relationship – and an issue of major importance in the context of this article – is whether the individual in question was, in fact, a traveller.

Must a guest be a traveller?

In many of the cases which revolve around the liability of hoteliers for the stolen property of guests, the courts do not directly address the issue of whether the person claiming to be a guest was, or should be, a traveller (see, for example, *Thompson v Lacy*[44] and *Bennett v Mellor*). This rather leads one to question whether an individual does in fact need to be a traveller to establish the host/guest relationship. Asquith L.J. commented on this quirk of the caselaw in *Williams v Linnitt*:[45]

> "There are decisions which, dealing with the rights of a guest, are silent on the question whether the person suing as guest was a traveller. There are no decisions which say expressly that anyone can be a guest without being a traveller, and [a number of] decisions, in my view, tacitly assume a guest to have fulfilled the qualification necessary to his becoming a guest, namely, that he should have been a traveller."

In fact, there is considerable authority to support the view that being a traveller has long been a prerequisite to being a guest. In *Williams v Linnitt* Asquith LJ went on to provide a useful review of the legal position up to that date. He said:

> "... I think it plain that a plaintiff is not a "guest" for the purpose of acquiring the peculiar remedies which the common law confers as against an innkeeper unless he be also a "traveller""

He explained that he believed the point to be established beyond question by the following among other considerations:

> "(i) The old writ, which in the time of Elizabeth: see *Calye's Case*; could alone initiate a claim of this kind, described the plaintiff or plaintiffs as "transiens" or "transeuntes". (ii) In the field of criminal prosecutions, for not "receiving" the prosecutor, the indictment was bad if it did not contain any allegation that the plaintiff was a traveller ... [see *R v Luellin*,[46] *R v Rymer*[47] and *R v Higgins*[48]] ... (iii) In the field of civil litigation, since

---

44   *(1820) 3 B & Ald 283*
45   *[1951] 1 All ER 278*
46   *88 ER 1441 (1701)*
47   *(1877) 2 QBD 136*
48   *[1948] 1 KB 165*

Calye's Case the allegation that the plaintiff was a "traveller" or "travelling" has been held an indispensable averment in the declaration."

Moreover, this view that a person must be a traveller before they can be considered to be a guest appears to be enshrined in the Hotel Proprietors' Act 1956 which now governs the area of hoteliers' liability for guests' property. The Act is evidently based on the common law, referring always to 'a traveller' or 'any traveller' as the person to whom obligations are owed by the hotelier. This can be seen clearly from sections 1(3) and 2(1) where it states:

1(3) In this Act, the expression "hotel" means an establishment held out by the proprietor as offering food, drink and, if so required, sleeping accommodation, without special contract, to any traveller presenting himself who appears able and willing to pay a reasonable sum for the services and facilities provided and who is in a fit state to be received.

2(1) Without prejudice to any other liability incurred by him with respect to any property brought to the hotel, the proprietor of an hotel shall not be liable as an innkeeper to make good to any traveller any loss of or damage to such property except where—

(a) at the time of the loss or damage sleeping accommodation at the hotel had been engaged for the traveller; and

(b) the loss or damage occurred during the period commencing with the midnight immediately preceding, and ending with the midnight immediately following, a period for which the traveller was a guest at the hotel and entitled to use the accommodation so engaged.

However, during the passage of the proposed Hotel Proprietors (Liabilities and Rights) Bill in the House of Lords there was considerable debate over whether the word 'traveller' should have been used or whether this would unnecessarily limit the application of the Act. Lord Silkin said:

> "I beg to move this Amendment, which is to substitute the word "person" for the word "traveller"... I do not know whether the term "traveller" is a term of art, or the subject of any legal definition, or whether, if it is, it is desired to confine the advantages of this Bill to a "traveller" as distinct from anybody else. But I think we ought to use the widest possible word ... Surely the noble Lord does not intend to confine himself to people who are described as travellers? If he does, ought he not to provide a definition of the word "traveller"? If he did, he would find that he was really a person."[49]

In fact, similar concerns to those of Lord Silkin had already been expressed in *Orchard v Bush*[50] by Kennedy J. regarding whether guests really needed to be 'travellers' to gain the protection of the law. He said:

> "I agree that, on the facts of this case, the plaintiff was a traveller; but apart from the question whether he was a traveller or not, I am of the opinion that if a man is in an inn for the purpose of receiving such accommodation as the innkeeper can give him, he is entitled to the protection the law gives to a guest at an inn."

Wills J. also made a similar point in the same case:

> "There is not much to be said upon the authorities, for the proposition that a person, in order to be a guest at the inn, must be a wayfarer or a traveller."

Furthermore, while the English texts on Hotel Law have little to say on the subject, one American text,[51] suggests that:

---

49   *Hansard, 19 June 1956 p.1074*

50   *[1898] 2 Q.B 284*

51   *Sherry, John EH, The Laws of Innkeepers, 3rd edition, 1993 Ithaca: Cornell University Press, p.114*

> "even a person not entitled to admittance, not being a bona
> fide traveller, will become a guest and entitled to the rights
> of a guest if he is received in the inn upon the same footing
> as a guest"

He cites the American case of *Walling v Potter*[52], and the English case
of *Orchard v Bush & Co* as authority for his point.

Ultimately it appears from the wording of the Act that Lord Silkin's
concerns were either allayed or not heeded. It seems that this was due
to two main things. Firstly, and as will be seen later, the whole purpose
of the Bill was to *narrow* the class of people to whom hoteliers would
be strictly liable to 'genuine travellers – that is, those who stay a night
at an inn or hotel', as Lord Merthyr put it. Secondly, if the word
"traveller" was used instead of the word "person", this would avoid a
situation where the Bill would conflict with the criminal law relating to
travellers. This is because in *R v Higgins*[53] the Court of Criminal
Appeal clearly decided that an innkeeper's duty under the criminal law
to supply refreshment did *not* extend to a person who could not be
regarded as a traveller.

Other concerns about the effectiveness of the Act were raised and
rebutted during the reading of the Bill. However, in the context of this
chapter, perhaps the most valid point made by Lord Silkin was when
he questioned why it was that if the Act dictated that a claimant must
be a traveller to succeed in a claim against an hotelier, why was the
expression 'traveller' not defined?

When does a traveller become a guest?

If we are to accept that the hotelier's strict common law duty to protect
belongings only extends to travellers, at what stage does a traveller
become a guest? For example in *Strauss v The County Hotel and Wine
Co Ltd*,[54] the plaintiff was clearly a traveller, but the court held that, as

---

52   *35 Conn. 183 (1868)*

53   *[1948] 1 KB 165*

54   *(1883) 12 QBD 27*

he had not become a guest at the hotel, he could not recover the value of his stolen belongings from the hotelier. Here, Lord Coleridge CJ said:

> "The law relating to the liability of innkeepers is fully considered in *Calye's Case* and it is clear that in order to make the innkeeper liable at common law the plaintiff must have been a guest at the inn."

Therefore, it is generally accepted that a traveller becomes a guest on having been *received* at an hotel/inn.

There is very little discussion in the English texts, and very few cases, on what it means to be received as a guest at an hotel. Moreover, the Hotel Proprietors Act 1956 offers little guidance. The Act tells us nothing about what it means to be received as a guest; it merely tells us that only a guest who stays the night will gain the protection of the common law principle of hoteliers' strict liability for guests' property. Presumably then, a guest must still be 'received' before an hotelier can become liable for their property under the Act and it must be assumed, therefore, that we must turn to the common law to determine whether or not someone has in fact been received as a guest.

Strauss v County Hotel and Wine Co Ltd is one of the few English cases which directly illustrates what it means to be received at an hotel. The plaintiff arrived at the station in Carlisle where he was met by one of the porters of the defendant's hotel (which adjoined the railway station). He intended to spend the night and gave his luggage to the porter asking him to take it to the hotel. However, having read a telegram that was waiting for him, he decided to dine and go straight on to Manchester. As the hotel coffee-room was not yet serving, he was directed to the station refreshment room. This was under the same management as the hotel and joined to it by a covered passage. On his way there, he met the porter and asked him to lock up his luggage until he was ready to go on to Manchester. Unfortunately, when it was time to leave, the plaintiff found that part of his luggage was missing.

The plaintiff suggested that the fact that the porter had received his luggage was recognition that he was a guest and he therefore claimed that the hotel was responsible for his stolen luggage. However, Mathew J. in finding for the defendant said:

> "The counsel for the plaintiff were called upon to shew at what point of time the relation of landlord and guest commenced. They suggested that it was when the plaintiff gave his luggage to the porter. But at that time the plaintiff had not made up his mind to become a guest. The fact that he ordered his goods locked up, and that they were locked up, is no more than if he said that he was uncertain whether he should stay in the inn, and that in the meantime he wished his goods to be locked up. In such a case there could be no liability."

Clearly then, announcing one's arrival as a hotel guest to a porter is not enough to establish the host/guest relationship. This is underlined, in the context of American Law, by Sherry[55] who notes that 'the burden appears to be on the applicant to give notice that he desires to be received as a guest'. He goes on to suggest that to become a guest in an hotel, a person must give the hotelier an opportunity to receive or reject him. This is supported by both the English case of *Hawthorne v Hammond*[56] and the much more recent US case of *Langford v Vandaveer*.[57]

In the former case, it was held that in order to be liable for not receiving a guest – in this case, at night – the innkeeper must have been made aware of the plaintiff knocking at the door. Similarly, in *Langford's* case a man in a group of two men and two women had asked for accommodation for "four oil men". When, subsequently, one of the women was seriously injured by the explosion of a gas heater in their room she failed to recover damages from the hotelier. She had claimed that she was a "lawful guest for pay", but as the hotelier had

---

55   At p.106
56   174 Eng. Rep. 866, 869 (1844)
57   254 S.W.2d 498 (Ky.1953)

never been made aware of her presence in the hotel, the appeal court held for the defendants. It was said:

> "... the intention of the young lady to become a guest in the legal sense is apparent. The question is whether or not she was intentionally or knowingly received as such by the proprietor of the motor court ... [A] person may not impose himself upon the proprietor and become a guest without his knowledge or intention to receive him. One becomes a guest only if he is received and treated as a guest and the intention to become such must be communicated to the innkeeper or his agent."

From these cases it is evident that before any person can be considered to be a guest at an hotel notice must be given and that giving notice to a porter is not enough. But, to whom should notice be given? Sherry suggests that notice should usually be given to an employee whose duty it is to receive or reject travellers, such as the receptionist or assistant manager. Nevertheless it is not necessary that there should be a *formal* bargain. Numerous cases suggest that the courts are willing to imply acceptance of a guest from the conduct of the parties. For example, in *Bennett v Mellor* (discussed more fully below) the mere fact that the plaintiff, a traveller, sat down and had a drink at the inn was considered enough to suggest that he had been received as a guest. Also in *Grant v Cardiff Hotels Company*[58] the fact that the plaintiff went to the lavatory to wash his hands appears to have given rise to the host/guest relationship. Here, the plaintiff recovered damages as a result of his purse disappearing from the pocket of the coat he had left in the lavatory although the theft occurred before he had even seen the innkeeper at all. In this case the plaintiff *subsequently* established the host/guest relationship by using the hotel's dining room. The relationship was held to operate retrospectively from the moment he came into the hotel.

However, it is such common practice today to announce one's arrival at the reception desk of an hotel that the problem of establishing when

---

58   *37 Times L. Rep.775 (1921)*

a person is received at an hotel is not likely to be much of an issue. Certainly, it would be very difficult to 'engage a room' without dealing with reception. Also, the 'lavatory' issue in *Grant v Cardiff* would now be covered by the fact that the 1956 Act only covers property stolen from guests who have engaged sleeping accommodation.[59]

Nevertheless grey areas remain. One particularly difficult area is the situation where individuals come to the hotel as 'sub-guests' or guests of other guests.

Guests of guests

In these situations can the host/guest relationship really be said to have arisen between the hotelier and the sub-guest? Moreover, can a sub-guest therefore really be considered to be a traveller in his or her own right? From the cases, the answer appears to be 'yes'. In *Wright v Anderton*[60] the Bradford hockey club reserved and paid for a room in a hotel in which the visiting team could change and then have tea after the match. Valuables were stolen from clothes in the room and the plaintiff, one of the visitors, sued the hotelier. The plaintiff claimed that although he had taken no food in the hotel when his belongings were stolen and had not paid for his room, he became a common law guest when he entered the hotel and was admitted by the hotelkeeper. The county court judge agreed that this was in fact the case.

Applying this principle it would appear that anyone who comes to an hotel room, which has been engaged for the night, but paid for by a third party, is covered as a guest on common law principles. Therefore, presumably, package tourists would automatically be covered as guests in a hotel despite the fact that their room had been arranged and paid for by a third party, the tour operator – although this raises other questions about whether individuals who have had their rooms arranged/contracted in advance can be considered to be bona fide travellers and hence guests (see 'Guest or Lodger?' below).

---

59   *Hotel Proprietors Act 1956 s2(1)*
60   *[1909] 1 KB 209*

Two other cases also support this decision. In *Gordon v Silber*[61] it was held that, although the arrangement for the hotel room was made with the husband, the hotel still had a lien over the wife's belongings. This was thought to be co-extensive with the innkeepers duties towards the wife as a guest. Also in *Cryan v Rembrandt Hotel*[62] it was held that a guest's visitor could recover the value of a valuable cloak which was stolen while she was with a friend in the hotel.

Refusal of guests

Finally, within the context of the host/guest relationship, it is worth mentioning that if the hotelier refuses to receive a person as a guest, whether lawful or not, the relationship is not established. In *White's Case*[63] an innkeeper refused to receive a person, because his inn was full. The plaintiff insisted on sharing with other guests and his belongings were subsequently stolen. In finding for the innkeeper the decision was reported as follows:

> "... [I]f a guest come to a common innkeeper to harbour there, and he say that his house is full of guests, and do not admit him, &c. and the party say he will make shift among other guests, and be there robbed of his goods, the innkeeper shall not be charged, because he refused the guest. And if the cause of the refusal be false, the guest may have an action on the case for his refusal."

It seems therefore that, with some exceptions, there are three ingredients to the guest/innkeeper relationship:

● The establishment in question must be an hotel (see Chapter One)

● The person resorting to the hotel must be a traveller

● The person must have been received as a guest at the hotel at the time their belongings were stolen

Unfortunately, as we have already indicated, the HPA does not define

---

61   *(1890) 25 QBD 491*
62   *(1925) 133 LT 395*
63   *73 ER 47, 343 (KB 1558)*

what is meant by the term traveller. Therefore to consider the meaning of the term we have to look in some detail at the development of the caselaw on this subject.

The Development of the Law

(a) A traveller is a transient person?

For hundreds of years, it has been considered that to be a traveller, in law, a person must be 'transient'. In the early cases, this was interpreted to mean someone on a journey from A to B; a wayfarer or a passenger. *Calye's case*, which sets out a number of 'rules' relating to innkeepers, reflects this approach:

> "The words are, *ad hospitandos homines per partes ubi hujusmodi hospitia existunt transeuntes, et in eisdem hospitantes*; by which it appears that common inns are instituted for passengers and wayfaring men...[a]nd therefore if a neighbour who is no traveller, as a friend, at the request of the innholder lodges there and his goods be stolen, etc. he shall not have an action ...".

The whole purpose of the common law relating to travellers and *'transeuntes'* was that it gave protection to strangers who, needing food and overnight shelter, turned up at an inn 'unannounced' or without having made any prior contract for their lodging. For this reason, the notion of a 'traveller' has always been inextricably entwined with the definition of an inn. Indeed, the definitions of 'traveller' and 'inn' are effectively two sides of the same coin (see Chapter One). For example, in *Thompson v Lacy*, Best J. attempts to define an inn by describing the type of visitor it was bound to receive:

> "An inn is a house, the owner of which holds out that he will receive all travellers and sojourners who are willing to pay a price adequate to the sort of accommodation provided, and who come in a situation in which they are fit to be received."

In the American case of *Bonner v Welborn*[64] Judge Nesbet said:

"It is because inns and innkeepers have to do with the travelling public – strangers – and that for brief periods, and under circumstances which render it impossible for each customer to contract for the terms of his entertainment, that the law has taken them so strictly in charge."

In s.1(3) of the Hotel Proprietors Act 1956, the definition of an hotel is also framed in terms of whom a hotel proprietor would expect to receive:

"In this Act, the expression "hotel" means an establishment held out by the proprietor as offering food, drink and, if so required, sleeping accommodation, without special contract, to any traveller presenting himself who appears able and willing to pay a reasonable sum for the services and facilities provided and who is in a fit state to be received."

It is clear from the above definitions that the general expectation of innkeepers was that they would receive *all* transients, that is, those who turned up on their doorstep. However, it is evident that there were limits to the type of traveller the hotelier was obliged to accommodate. Travellers were expected to be in a fit state to be received and to be able to pay a reasonable sum. (These and other exceptions to the hoteliers duty to accommodate are considered in more detail in a later chapter). There are also individuals who visit or stay in hotels who clearly fall outside the category of 'transient' or traveller and therefore have no special common law rights. These are considered later in this chapter.

However if we are to accept that to be a traveller is to be transient or on a journey this raises a number of questions as to who falls within this class. For example, how far from home must a person have travelled to be considered transient? How long can an individual stay

---

64   *7 Ga.296 (1849)*

in one place and still be transient? Can visits arranged in advance as opposed to ad hoc visits be regarded as transient visits?

To an extent, these, and a number of other issues have been addressed by caselaw over the years – and more recently by statute. However, as will be seen, a precise definition of a traveller, in a legal sense, remains elusive.

(b) The changing concept of a traveller: from overnight guest to temporary visitor?

The traveller as overnight guest

In the very early cases of the 16th and early 17th Centuries, it was considered that to be a traveller – and hence to benefit from the public duties of innkeepers – a person had to stay the night or at least engage a room for the night at an inn[65]. Otherwise, a person visiting the inn was considered to be a mere 'tippler'. As Coke CJ said in that case:

> "... and if a neighbour of the innkeeper come to the innkeeper, he shall not answer for the goods, for he is not lodged, but as a tipler [sic], and so if an innkeeper invite any to his house *ad prandendum aut caenandum*, the innkeeper shall not be charged ..."

This test that a man must stay the night in order to be considered a traveller had real merit. It was clear and simple to apply and, for a busy innkeeper, it effectively surmounted the problem of attempting to establish who was a traveller by other more difficult means. It was also a good test, for who, other than a traveller from outside the area, in an age when leisure time and holidays were practically non-existent, would stay the night at an inn?

However, by 1793 this simple test to ascertain who was and who was not a traveller had been lost and subsequent caselaw decisions significantly broadened the definition of traveller. This meant that it became unnecessary to stay for even one night at an inn in order to be considered a traveller.[66]

---

65   *Warbrooke v Griffin (1609) 2 Br & G 254*

66   *York v Grindstone (1703), 2 Ld Raym 866*

The traveller as temporary visitor

Bennett v Mellor is the leading case which established that a person could still benefit from the protection afforded to travellers even if he didn't stay overnight. However, it was *York v Grindstone* which paved the way for this decision when it was decided that, because he left his horse at an inn, Mr Grindstone's property would be protected by the common law despite the fact that he didn't stay the night there himself.

In *Bennett v Mellor*[67] – a case in which goods were stolen from an inn – the facts of the case are reported as:

'… [T]he plaintiff's servant had taken the goods in question to market at Manchester, and not being able to dispose of them went with them to the defendant's inn, and asked the defendant's wife if he could leave the goods there till the week following [meaning the next market day]; she said she could not tell, for they were very full of parcels. The plaintiff's servant sat down in the inn, had some liquor, and put the goods on the floor immediately behind him. When he got up, after sitting there a little while, the goods were missing.'

In finding a verdict for the plaintiff, Buller, J. 'considered this to be the common case of goods brought into an inn by a guest, and stolen from thence, in which case the innkeeper was liable to make good the loss.' *Calye's case* was cited as authority for the decision and the effect of *Bennett v Mellor* was strongly supported by JW Smith in 1837[68] where in his notes on *Calye's Case* he writes:

"It is not necessary, in order that a man should be a guest, so as to fix the innkeeper with liability, that he should have come for more than temporary refreshment."

This view has not been challenged in any subsequent editions of Smith's 'Leading Cases' and is widely accepted as good law.[69]

---

67   *5 Term Rep 273; 101 ER 154 (1793); 29 Digest 12, 162*
68   *1 Sm LC 10th ed., p.124*
69   *Orchard v Bush; Williams v Linnitt*

The effect of *Bennett v Mellor* was that a traveller could demand temporary refreshment at an inn and, if received, gain the benefit of protection for property at common law which had previously only been owed by innkeepers to travellers who stayed overnight. In other words, where a traveller stopped at an inn to get refreshment, and was received, even if temporarily and despite having no intention of staying the night, this would be enough to give rise to the innkeeper/guest relationship.

The decision in *Bennett v Mellor* therefore led to the end of a clear distinction between who could be considered to be a traveller in the eyes of the law and who could not. For example, if a traveller was no longer someone who stayed the night or sought to stay the night how would an innkeeper or hotelier distinguish a local 'tippler' from a traveller and therefore recognise the different obligations and duties owed to each? This raised a variety of questions for the courts, particularly as counsel for the defence now sought to narrow the definition of traveller in other ways. For example, they argued that the manner in which visitors used inns, or that the distance or way they travelled, meant they couldn't be considered travellers. *Orchard v Bush & Co* decided over 100 years later, illustrates the point very well.

In that case, the plaintiff, a man returning home from work in Liverpool one evening, called in for supper at an hotel en route to the train station. On leaving after dinner, he found that his overcoat had been stolen. Counsel for the defence contended that, firstly, for the hotel to be liable for the man's property, he must be a traveller at the time his belongings were stolen. Secondly, that he was not, on the facts, a traveller as he had only used the hotel as a restaurant. Counsel attempted to argue that while the plaintiff in *Bennett v Mellor* was 'clearly a traveller', the plaintiff in the current case was not. On appeal, Wills J. was of the view that he was indeed a traveller:

> "It is said that in order to make him a guest he must be a wayfarer and traveller. The facts are that he was on his way home; he was on his way to the station from which he travelled home by railway. Why was he not a wayfarer?

If he had been riding to his home on horseback along a country road, and between the *terminus a quo* and the *terminus ad quem* he used an inn for the purpose of getting food for himself and his horse, he clearly would be a wayfarer and a guest at the inn. What difference does it make that he was not riding, as 100 years ago he probably would have been, but that he was walking to the railway station in order to take the train, and on the way called at an inn, and was received there and served with such refreshment as he required? I think a guest is a person who uses the inn, either for a temporary or more permanent stay, in order to take what the inn can give. He need not stay the night."

Kennedy J. concurred, attempting to define a traveller as follows:

"The authorities give no definition of what is a traveller; but looking at the reason of the thing, I should have thought that any person, who was neither an inhabitant of the house nor a private guest of the innkeeper or his family, but who came into the house as a guest to get such accommodation as it afforded and he was willing to pay for, was a traveller. It does not seem to me to make any difference whether his journey be a long or a short one."

The judgments in this case make it clear that distance and means of travel could not necessarily be used to successfully distinguish between a traveller and a non-traveller. Moreover, they underlined that, while the principles of the common law were founded in a pre-industrial era with pre-industrial means of transport, they applied equally to a much more contemporary scenario.

Therefore, from the middle ages to the turn of the 20th century, the courts had allowed the concept of the traveller to broaden radically. A traveller was no longer simply a wayfarer, usually on horseback, who stayed overnight as part of a 'traditional' journey but now encompassed the 'modern-day' commuter who might stop for a bite to eat on the way home or, to paraphrase Wills J, to take what the hotel can give. In fact, as evidenced by Kennedy J's definition above, a traveller had, with a few exceptions, become almost 'any person'.

Certainly, it could be argued that, in today's context, travel is such a commonplace phenomenon that we are all travellers, every day, and that trying to distinguish a 'traveller' from any other person is almost impossible.

This point was given further weight in *Williams v Linnitt* another case in which the court had to address the issue of whether a person who used an hotel for only temporary refreshment could be deemed a traveller.

In *Williams v Linnitt*, the facts were that John Frederick Williams, a farmer, drove back from Nuneaton towards home one evening. However, when he reached his house, rather than stopping there, he continued one mile further on to the Royal Red Gate Inn to meet some friends there for a drink. Having parked his car at the front of the inn, he spent about an hour there, but when he came outside he found that his car had been stolen. Williams successfully brought an action against the proprietor of the inn for damages for the loss of the car.

On appeal against a judgment made for the plaintiff, the defendant argued, among other things, that the plaintiff did not fall within the common law definition of a "traveller". He argued that whatever the meaning of a traveller might be:

> "... it was sufficient for his purpose to contend that the word did not include a person residing in the immediate neighbourhood who leaves his home for the sole purpose of drinking with his friends and then returning home again". (p.279)

There is certainly authority for the point that local residents could not be considered to be travellers: see, for example *R v Rymer* and *R v Higgins*. However, these cases, which were criminal prosecutions brought against proprietors for failure to receive, were not followed.

Instead, it was held that 'although the plaintiff was residing in the immediate neighbourhood of the inn and visited it merely to take a drink, he was ... a "traveller" for the purposes of establishing the defendant's liability as an innkeeper at common law'. The judgments of Lord Tucker, Asquith LJ and Denning LJ provide a detailed overview and 'potted history' of the law relating to the definition of a traveller and all come to the same conclusion. Within this, *Orchard v Bush* is cited as strong authority for their decision. Asquith LJ sums this up:

> "... in *Orchard v Bush & Co*, the plaintiff was held entitled to enforce the special obligations resting on an innkeeper when he stopped at the inn for a meal when en route from his office in Liverpool to his residence some miles outside it. I cannot persuade myself that, if this is so, a person who travels to an inn from his own residence for a meal and a drink and travels back to his own residence afterwards, is not a traveller also."

However, Denning had a certain amount of sympathy with the view of counsel for the defence. He cited a number of cases where a man popping into an inn for a drink would indeed have been dismissed as a mere 'tippler' and would not have been entitled to the status of traveller[70] Nevertheless he appears to dismiss the view that the plaintiff was a mere tippler for 'common sense' reasons:

> "Once it is accepted that a man, who comes for temporary refreshment while on a journey, is a traveller, there is no practical way of distinguishing him from the local resident ... [T]he courts have opened the door of the inn to the man who stops for a drink on his way home, and, once he gets his foot in, the door cannot be shut against the local resident, for it is beyond the wit of man to know one from the other. In the course of the argument, Asquith LJ put the case of two men walking home from work. Both go to the same inn for a drink, but the home of one is on the hither side of it and the home of the other is on the further

---

70   *Warbrooke v Griffin; Pidgeon v Legg; R v Rymer; R v Higgins.*

side. Is one a traveller and the other not? Such illustrations convince me that we cannot accept the contention of counsel for the defendant and we must hold the plaintiff to be a traveller."

This decision, seemingly harsh on hotel proprietors, was one of the last in a series of common law decisions that led to what hoteliers considered to be an unjust situation. Now, hoteliers could find themselves liable for a guest's property as a result of the briefest of visits. Moreover, the class of individual who enjoyed this right had grown to include almost any person walking through the door of the hotel.

The Hotel Proprietors Act 1956 was subsequently enacted specifically to modify the liabilities and rights of innkeepers – largely in their favour – and, in doing so, it significantly affected who could and who could not be considered to be a traveller/guest.

Travellers and the Hotel Proprietors Act 1956

The main points of contention for hoteliers regarding the development of the common law were twofold. First, they considered there to be an unfair distinction between themselves and the owners of private hotels, restaurants and public houses in respect of the burden imposed on them regarding their liability for travellers' possessions. They felt this especially in relation to those travellers who merely called in for a meal or a drink. Secondly, in an age when car ownership and use was becoming quite commonplace, it was felt to be unfair that they should carry the burden of strict responsibility for guests' cars, particularly in the light of guests' temporary and sometimes fleeting use of their hotel's facilities.

Therefore, when the Law Reform Committee (LRC) was appointed in 1952 to consider what changes might be 'desirable in the law relating to innkeeper's liability in respect of the property of travellers, guests and residents', the Committee agreed with some, although not all, of these representations. They would not, for example, follow the view that the principle of strict liability of hoteliers/innkeepers should be removed completely. As the findings of the LRC put it:

"... [T]he fact that a new class of residential hotels and similar places has grown up does not seem to us to be a valid reason for abolishing the old rule. The traveller is today as much as in the past exposed to the risk of loss through neglect on the part of the innkeeper or his servants ..."71

However, they did recommend that legislative provision should be made not only to remove hoteliers' strict liability for guests' cars, but also to limit their strict liability for travellers/guests belongings to those who stayed overnight:

"We see no reason why the law should not return to its old conception of a traveller as one who stays the night at the inn or hotel, except that we would include any person by or for whom a bedroom is engaged. If this were done, it would remove the unsatisfactory distinction under the existing law between the position of the person who takes a meal at a restaurant and one who dines out at an 'inn'" (p.6)

This recommendation was subsequently incorporated into the 1956 Act at section 2(1) as indicated above.

However, it is questionable whether, as the LRC suggested, the 1956 Act has really either reversed or supplanted the common law notion of a traveller. The 1956 Act merely confines the right of recovering the value of property stolen at an hotel to those travellers who stay (or who plan to stay) overnight, among other things. As no definition is given, it must be assumed that whether a person is a traveller or not still depends on the common law. It was argued in the Solicitors' Journal72 that the Act in fact, created two tiers of traveller:

---

71 *Law Reform Committee, Second Report, Innkeepers' Liability for Property of Travellers, Guests and Residents, 1954, Cmnd 9161, p.6*
72 *The Solicitors' Journal, Saturday February 9, 1957, Vol. 101 p.137*

"A practical effect of this new form of limitation on the innkeeper's absolute liability is to create two classes of traveller. First, there is the customer who, in pursuance of the "holding out" and of the common law, can insist on being provided with refreshment or accommodation according to his requirements and to the resources which the host may reasonably have available. Whether he has booked sleeping accommodation does not matter, and on the basis of *Williams v Linnitt* [1951] 1 KB 565 it is also immaterial whether he is a needy wayfarer or a local resident. The proprietor renders himself liable to proceedings on indictment if he refuses without reasonable excuse to provide what is required. But only to travellers who have booked a bedroom will mine host in future be liable, as an innkeeper, for any mischance affecting their property."

Another approach is to say that there have always been two tiers of traveller: 'traveller' and 'guest' and that the Act simply amends the concept of 'guest' from one who has been received at an hotel to mean one who stays overnight. Pannet & Boella[73] appear to take this view, suggesting that "the term guest is used to describe a traveller who has taken sleeping accommodation at the inn. Hence a traveller becomes a guest upon taking one night's sleeping accommodation". In any case, neither of these suggestions deal with 'who is a traveller' and contrary to the suggestion of the Law Reform Committee, the Act does not state that a traveller is a person who stays overnight. Instead, it appears to leave this open.

In other words although it is now clear that a necessary requisite for enjoying the protection of property during a stay at an hotel is an overnight stay, can this be a *sufficient* requirement for a person to merit status as a traveller? There are, for example, individuals who meet the requirement of staying overnight in an hotel but are not travellers. These include those who have stayed overnight in an hotel but who

---

73   *Principles of Hospitality Law, 2nd ed., 1999, p.147*

have never been classed as travellers, for example, invited guests of the hotelier *(Calye)* or permanent lodgers; there are also those who have stayed so long at an hotel that they have ceased to be a traveller; these points are dealt with below.

Non-travellers

From earliest times it has been accepted that not every person who goes to an inn is a traveller. *Calye's case* provides one of the earliest examples of this:

> "[i]f a neighbour, who is no traveller, as a friend at the request of the innkeeper lodges there and his goods be stolen, &c. he shall not have an action."

In *Orchard v Bush*, 1898, Kennedy J. also specifically singled out 'private guest[s] of the innkeeper or his family' as being excluded from the definition as well as 'inhabitant[s] of the house' and later, in *Williams v Linnitt*, Asquith J. lists those whom he considers to be excluded from the term "traveller" as being:

> "(a) the innkeeper's family living in the inn, (b) the innkeeper's servants, (c) the innkeeper's private guests, (d) lodgers at the inn, and (e) persons resorting to the inn for purposes unconnected with the enjoyment of the facilities which it provides as an inn – for example, to repair the drains or to sell the innkeeper a sewing machine."

Pannett & Boella also take this approach, listing friends of the innkeeper, repair people and traders, salespeople and company representatives, long-term guests and delivery people as those who, when visiting hotels for purposes other than to use it as such, are non-travellers.

Theoretically, non-travellers cannot enjoy the protection of the common law if, during their visit to an hotel, their belongings are stolen. However, in practice there will always be grey areas. One might envisage a situation where, for example, a salesperson, having concluded the day's business, might stay for the night as a guest in the hotel. In the same way, a friend of an hotelier might have been invited for a meal, but became an ordinary paying hotel guest for his or her overnight stay. In practice, under the current law, it is never going to be easy for an hotelier to distinguish between 'travellers' and 'non-travellers'. This situation is only made more complicated by the fact that it is possible that individuals who are received as travellers, can lose their status as such, depending on their length of stay.

Length of stay as affecting the status of a traveller

In the early days, length of stay was a determining factor in whether a person could be considered to be 'transient' or a traveller. It was thought that to stay too long meant that a person would lose their status as a traveller and become a 'boarder'. In the early cases it appears that only a very short stay was acceptable. See, for example, *Gulielm's Case*[74] where it was suggested that the length of time which a person could stay and retain their status as a traveller was only one, two or three days. It was also thought worthy of mention in the notes to *Whites Case*[75] that 'lawyers at the assizes and gentlemen at the horse races occasionally stayed more than three nights and were still considered to be travellers'. Likewise in *Harland's Case*[76] the court discussed whether a man could still be considered to be a traveller after fourteen days. However, as time progressed it became evident that there were many occasions where a person could stay at an inn for a reasonably lengthy period and still be considered to be a traveller. As Scholl J. points out, in *Daniel v Pacific Pty*:[77]

> "... a series of decisions has established, contrary to the supposed older law, that a person may remain a long time a guest – *Thompson v Lacy* (eighty-three nights); *Allen v Smith*, (1862) 12 C.B. (N.S.) 638 (seven months); *Robins & Co v Gray*, [1895] 2 Q.B. 501 (four months); *Chesham*

---

74 *(1625), Lat 88, 82 ER 288*
75 *(1558) 2 Dyer, 158b*
76 *(1641), Clay 97, 29 Digest 5, 42*
77 *[1953] ALR 1043*

Automobile Supply Ltd v Beresford Hotel (Birchington) Ltd., (1913) 29 T.L.R. 584 (four months)."

Notwithstanding this, the Court of Appeal case of *Lamond v Richard and the Gordon Hotels, Ltd*[78] clearly established the point that one of the ingredients in determining whether an individual could still be considered to be a traveller was the length of time they had stayed at an hotel.

In this case the plaintiff arrived at the Hotel Metropole in Brighton in November 1896 and remained in the hotel until August 31, 1897. She was reputedly a lady of good position and good character and paid her bill regularly. However, following complaints about her by other residents of the hotel, the under-manager enquired as to how long she was intending to stay in the hotel. Following her reply that she should stay as long as she liked, the under-manager gave her two days notice to leave, which she ignored. Six days later she was told that she must leave. As she didn't comply, when she went out for a walk her belongings were packed up and put in the hall. She claimed that, as she was a traveller when she arrived at the hotel, the relation of host and guest had been established and, as such, the host could not terminate that relationship without good reason and without her agreement as a guest. She argued that nothing had happened to change the character in which she originally came to the hotel and that lapse of time was not sufficient to change the relationship initially established between the parties. Nonetheless judgment was made for the defendants. It was held that:

> "the plaintiff had long ceased to be a traveller or wayfarer in the ordinary sense and had become a boarder or lodger, and that the defendants were entitled to determine the relation between themselves and the plaintiff on giving her reasonable notice"

In upholding this decision in the court of appeal, Chitty L.J. said:

> "The custom of England does not extend to persons who

---

78   *[1897] 1 QB 541*

are in an inn as lodgers or boarders, and the length of time that a guest has stayed is a material ingredient in determining such a question ... If the character of traveller is continuous it would follow that the plaintiff would have the right to reside at the hotel all her life, provided she conformed to the regulations and paid her bills, but that she could leave at any moment, while the landlord would be bound to provide lodging without any power to give her notice to leave. This is a startling proposition, and, as it is moreover unsupported by authority, I cannot assent to it."

In *Williams v Linnitt*, these early decisions were interpreted to suggest that if a guest stayed for more than three nights, he lost his status as a traveller and became a boarder. However, the validity of this interpretation of these cases has since been questioned (see the judgement of Scholl J in *Daniel v Pacific*).

Guest or lodger?

It is clear that lodgers or boarders are not generally considered to be travellers and, as such, have no common law rights in respect of protection for their property, only contractual ones. But how is the distinction between who is a guest and who is a lodger to be made? Length of stay is one factor, but as discussed above, this is not decisive. In fact, the major difference between the two appears to be that a lodger makes a definite contractual arrangement with the hotelier to stay for a period of time, whereas a traveller will show up 'on spec'.

This principle was established from a growing body of law during the seventeenth and eighteenth centuries which suggested that a person who "boarded" at an inn was 'outside the custom'. In a note to *Calye's case*[79] it was said:

> "If a man hires a chamber for a term, *Warbrooke v Griffiths*, Moore 876, ... the innkeeper is not chargeable".

---

79   *At p.521*

Drope v Theyar,[80] *Grimston v An Innkeeper,*[81] and *Parker v Flint*[82] provide similar authority for the point

In *Thompson v Lacy* , Best J. makes the distinction between a lodging house and an inn as follows:

> "A lodging-house keeper ... makes a contract with every man that comes; whereas an innkeeper is bound, without making any special contract, to provide lodging and entertainment for all, at a reasonable price."

Together, these decisions were reflected in Bacon's "Inns and Innkeepers",[83] where it states:

> "But if A comes with goods to an inn in London, and stays there for a week, month or longer, and is there robbed of them, he shall have an action against his host ... But if an attorney hires a chamber in an inn for the whole term, he is quasi a lessee, and if robbed, the host is not answerable (Moor 877). So, if a man upon special agreement boards or sojourns in an inn, and is robbed, the host shall not answer for it (Latch 127; Hetley 49)."

However, this means of distinguishing between lodgers and travellers does not sit easily with modern ways of travel. Today, an individual is more likely than not to telephone a busy hotel in advance to secure a room, giving a credit card number or sending a deposit. Strangely enough, it seems that by doing so, under existing law, a person is making a special contractual arrangement which may deprive them of their rights to protection of property as a traveller at common law; a situation which appears to be paradoxical.

Nonetheless, as recently as 1953, in the case *of Daniel v Hotel Pacific*, the majority decision of the court, relying on the above-stated

---

80   *(1626) Poph. 178 at p.179,*

81   *(1627) Het. 49 124 ER 334*

82   *(1699) 12 Mod. 254; 88 ER 1303*

83   *7th ed., 1832, Vol. IV, p.448*

authorities, was as follows:

> "At common law a person who books accommodation at
> an hotel beforehand for a fixed period and who afterwards
> enters and is received on the basis of the arrangement is
> not a "guest" and the hotelkeeper is not liable as an insurer
> in respect of that person's goods while he is staying in the
> hotel".

The facts of this case were that the plaintiffs, fifteen of them altogether, had stayed at the Pacific Hotel in Lorne – a well known seaside resort in Australia – over Christmas and the New Year, 1950–51. The defendants, undisputedly innkeepers, operated an accommodation booking list for this period and all the plaintiffs, who lived some distance away, reserved their accommodation in advance, by telephone or letter, for definite periods from nine days to three weeks. On the 27th December, the hotel safe was stolen, containing the plaintiffs' money, which had been given to the hotelier for safe-keeping.

The plaintiffs claimed that under common law, the hotelier was strictly liable for their belongings as they were guests in the hotel. However, counsel for the defence contended that they were never received as guests in the hotel and that they were in fact lodgers as a result of the implied pre-existing contract between them and the hotelier. Two of the three judges in court agreed. However, Scholl J, dissenting, seriously questioned the reasoning behind their judgments. In doing so he presented a detailed and convincing argument as to what *discrimina* (as he put it) exist which provide a test to determine whether 'inmates' at an hotel are lodgers or guests/travellers.

He identifies four main questions to look at in cases such as these, which also provide a useful framework around which to discuss this issue:

1. Was there an antecedent contract?

In the early days of 'travel' it was considered extremely unusual indeed for a traveller to have arranged accommodation in advance. Above all, the means did not exist by which a traveller could do this. Therefore, it could be argued that making a contract for accommodation for a stated period was so unusual as to make such behaviour inconsistent with the ordinary use of inns and hence 'outside the custom', which would make the judgments above make sense, in their context.

However, the question to be asked here is whether principles founded upon a different age of travel can or should be applied without adaptation to a modern society? As we have seen, historically, the development of the law up to the mid 1950s appears to have allowed for changes in ways of travel while maintaining the intended spirit of the common law. Yet the decision in *Daniel v Pacific* appears to give little or no consideration to modern practice. As Scholl J. puts it:

"The first question for us, I think is whether we are to decide this case by applying to the plaintiffs tests which were or may have been apt in the seventeenth century to distinguish between the ordinary traveller's use of an inn and the use made of it by a person then regarded as a "boarder", or tests apt at the present time to distinguish between persons who use inns in the ordinary modern way of travellers or transients, and those who use them in a different way as persons nowadays considered "boarders" or "lodgers". In my opinion, the Courts in modern times have tended to adopt the latter approach, as being more in keeping with the maintenance of the law as a living force, capable of being adapted to the changing circumstances of society. Nor is that course, I think, inconsistent with the fact that an innkeeper's liability to his guest arises from the ancient custom of the realm of England, with a view to the protection of those who came "guestwise" to inns. That did not mean, and does not mean, that in order to be a guest a person must come to an inn in circumstances precisely similar to those which existed when the custom originated, for if it were so, the custom would long since have died out. If one sought, for example, to limit it today to travellers who arrive unannounced at hotels, demand accommodation, and demand to stay until they are ready to leave, there would be few cases indeed in any city of consequence in which liability under the custom would attach. But the custom is sufficiently and properly applied if applied to those who from time to time come "guestwise" to inns, in accordance with the manners of the day."

Three modern English cases can be found which imply that an antecedent contract is not necessarily inconsistent with the relationship of innkeeper and guest. In *Wright v Anderton* the Bradford Hockey Club had arranged the room in advance and yet those who used it were still considered to be guests. In *Constantine v Imperial Hotels*[84] the plaintiff was held entitled to recover damages for not being received at an inn. Judgment must have been made for him on the basis that at common law he could sue for refusal to receive him as a guest and this was despite the fact that he had made a previous agreement for his room. Finally, in *R v Higgins*, the court did not think it inconsistent with the plaintiff's status as a traveller that he had given antecedent notice of his intention to stop at an inn for a meal.

Despite this, *Daniel v Pacific* leaves us with a precedent, which suggests that the existence of a pre-existing contract between a person and an hotel confers the status of lodger on that person. The unsatisfactory nature of this result can be illustrated by considering the scenario of two friends and neighbours going on holiday to the same hotel over the same period. If one has the foresight to book his room ahead while the other does not, and their luggage is stolen while in the hotel, the prudent friend will be deprived of recovery while his more casual neighbour will be compensated as a traveller/guest!

In all cases, the question of whether a person is guest or a lodger is one of fact to be decided depending upon the circumstances, but a second potential distinction is thought to be the way in which the room is paid for.

---

84   *[1944] 2 All ER 171*

2. Was there fixing and payment of a non-daily rate?

In two early English cases, *Drope v Theyar* and *Thompson v Lacy*, it was thought that weekly or monthly payments for accommodation were evidence that a person was a boarder, as opposed to a lodger who paid at a daily rate. However, in two subsequent cases[85] where the respective plaintiffs attempted to show that they were guests and not lodgers, the judges made statements to indicate that paying for accommodation per week was not inconsistent with the relationship of innkeeper and guest. There is also a suggestion in the American caselaw[86] that:

> "the fact that payment for accommodation is made at a fixed rate per week, month or the like is merely one of the circumstances entitled to consideration, and accordingly it seems to be well settled that such a matter of payment is not of itself sufficient to change the ordinary relation of innkeeper and guest, and constitute the accommodated person a boarder or lodger ...".

3. Was an arrangement made for a definite period?

This issue has not been dealt with in any detail in the English cases. However, this issue of express agreements as to length of stay has been explored in detail in the US.[87] Unfortunately, the US cases do not give a definitive answer on the point. However, in his judgment in *Daniel*, Scholl J. does single out two particular cases which appear to demonstrate that an agreement to stay for a definite period of time was not necessarily thought to be inconsistent with the status of guest. In *Metzger v Schnabel*[88] the court said:

> "A special agreement fixing in advance the price to be paid, or the length of the stay, does not absolutely disturb the

---

85   *Alldis v Huxley (1891) 12 NSWR (L.) 158, and Chesham Automobile Supply Ltd. v Beresford Hotel (Birchington) Ltd, (1913) 29 TLR. 584*

86   *In a note to Fisher v Bonneville Hotel Co, (1920) 12 Am. L.R. Ann. 255, at pp. 261–3, written in 1921*

87   *See p.1057 of Daniel for the authorities cited there.*

88   *(1898) 52 N.Y. Supp. 105, cited 12 Am. L.R. Ann. at p.262.*

relation of innkeeper and guest, and constitute the person so acting a boarder or lodger."

Also in *Pinkerton v Woodward*,[89] the plaintiff, intending to embark upon a boat journey, stayed for two weeks at an hotel waiting for the boat to set sail. He didn't book passage on the boat until after he had secured his accommodation. The court said:

> "A traveller who enters an inn as a guest does not cease to be a guest by proposing to remain a given number of days, or by ascertaining the price that will be charged for his entertainment, or by paying in advance for the whole of the entertainment ... We see no reason why the innkeeper may not require payment in advance, or why the guest may not pay in advance for lodgings for a part or all the time he intends to remain a guest at the inn."

4. Was there apparent permanence of residence combined with the absence of any other permanent home?

One final 'common sense' test which has been applied in both the Australian and American courts to differentiate between guests and lodgers is whether there is evidence that the plaintiff has taken up apparent permanent residency at the hotel combined with the lack of a permanent home elsewhere. This point would seem to be glaringly obvious and yet it does not appear to have been applied in any of the reported English or Commonwealth cases other than in the dissenting judgment of Scholl J. in *Daniel v Pacific.*

Overall, there is little doubt that the current law regarding the legal status of guests, travellers and lodgers is unsatisfactory. Clarification and simplification of the law is clearly necessary. Unfortunately, the Hotel Proprietors Act 1956 fell far short of achieving this aim.

Perhaps the best advice to hoteliers is that given by Pannet and Boella which is, given the difficulties of establishing who is a traveller and who isn't, that they should just assume that everyone walking through the door is a traveller.

---

89   *(1867) 33 Cal. 557, 91 Am. Dec. 657, cited 12 Am. L.R. Ann., at p.262*

CHAPTER THREE
THE HOTELKEEPER'S RIGHT TO REJECT OR EJECT GUESTS. NO ROOM AT THE INN

In his book, *Colour Bar*,[90] the famous West Indian cricketer, Learie Constantine, later Lord Constantine, described how, in 1943 at the height of the war, he was turned away from the Imperial Hotel in London because of his colour. Although he had taken the precaution of telephoning in advance and informing the hotel that he was black he was nevertheless told when he arrived that if he stayed the night his bags would be put out in the morning and he would not be permitted to stay the full four nights that he had booked. The manageress said to his companion "We will not have niggers in the hotel because of the Americans. If they stay tonight, their luggage will be put out tomorrow and the doors locked." Apparently when he had entered the hotel someone had said: "The Imperial is coming to something if you're going to take niggers in!" Subsequently he sued the hotel and in the famous case *Constantine v Imperial Hotels Ltd*[91] the Court reaffirmed the ancient principle of English common law that, subject to limited exceptions, an hotel has to accept all comers. This despite the fact that in 1943 England had no race discrimination laws and would not have for over 30 years.

In the light of cases such as *Constantine* this article examines the obligation of the hotelkeeper to receive all comers and the extent to which he can refuse to receive travellers or to eject them after they have become guests.

---

90   *'Colour Bar'*, Learie Constantine, Stanley Paul, 1954
91   *[1944] 1 KB 693*

A right to be received

We have already seen in previous chapters that an hotelkeeper is, by definition, under a duty to receive all comers. In *Thompson v Lacy*[92] for instance Best J said:

> "An inn is a house, the owner of which holds out that he will receive all travellers and sojourners who are willing to pay a price adequate to the sort of accommodation provided, and who come in a situation in which they are fit to be received."

In *Medawar v Grand Hotel Co*[93] Lord Esher MR said:

> "An hotel-keeper by opening his house as an hotel offers it to the use of the public as such, and thereupon the common law of England imposes on him certain duties and give him certain rights. He has no right to refuse to take into his house any one of the public who offers himself as a guest, if he has room for him in his house ..."

Bowen LJ said in the same case that:

> "We start with this, that a man who comes to an hotel, if there is an unoccupied room, has a right to use that room."

In *Browne v Brandt*[94] Lord Alverstone CJ said:

> "The true view is, in my opinion, that an innkeeper may not pick and choose his guests; he must give the accommodation he has to persons who come to the inn as travellers for rest and refreshment."

---

92   *3 B & A 283 (1820)*
93   *[1891] 2 QB 11 (CA)*
94   *[1902] 1 KB 696*

The origins of this duty are discussed in some detail in the Scottish case, *Rothfield v North British Railway Co*[95] in the judgment of Lord Anderson:[96]

"... at an early date, the law laid it upon the innkeeper to perform this primary function as a matter of obligation. In some of the cases the underlying principle of the decisions which established this rule of law is said to be "public trust" or "public duty". I have no doubt, however, that the considerations on which the decisions are based are just these: travellers ought not to be compelled to sleep on the highways or in the fields. Private hospitality might fail them. There might be no private house available, or the occupier might be churlish. The monastery might be fully occupied. There remained the inn – the public house – which had originated in a purpose of entertaining travellers. This was obviously the institution in which a traveller should have the power of demanding necessary accommodation."

A similar rationale is expressed by Wyman:[97]

"The innkeeper is in a common calling under severe penalty if he does not serve all that apply, while the ordinary shopkeeper is in a private calling free to refuse to sell if he is so minded. The surrounding circumstances must again explain the origin of this unusual law. When the weary traveller reaches the wayside inn in the gathering dusk, if the host turn him away what shall he do? Go on to the next inn? It is miles away, and the roads are infested with robbers. The traveller would be at the mercy of the

---

95 1920 SC 805. *Although a Scottish case the court pointed out that the law of Scotland was the same as English law on this issue.*

96 *Lord Anderson's judgment was overruled by the higher court but his comments on this matter remain of relevance.*

97 *'The Law of the Public Callings as a Solution of the Trust Problem', Bruce Wyman, (1903) 17 Harvard LR 156.*

innkeeper, who might practise upon him any extortion, for the guest would submit to anything almost, rather than be put out into the night. Truly a special law is required to meet this situation, for the traveller is so in the hands of the innkeeper that only an affirmative law can protect him."

On the face of it this gives any traveller the right simply to turn up at the door of the hotel and demand entry and the hotelkeeper cannot refuse. However it should be evident from the statements above that this right to demand entry is not unqualified. There must be room at the hotel, the guest must be willing to pay a reasonable price and must be in a fit condition to be received.

Much of this has been incorporated in statute. It follows from the definition of an hotel found in the Hotel Proprietors Act 1956 that a traveller presenting himself at an hotel has the right to be received, but that right is also subject to certain limitations of the kind just mentioned:

> S.1(3) In this Act, the expression "hotel" means an establishment held out by the proprietor as offering food, drink and, if so required, sleeping accommodation, without special contract, to any traveller presenting himself who appears able and willing to pay a reasonable sum for the services and facilities provided and who is in a fit state to be received.

What follows is a discussion of the circumstances in which the hotelkeeper can justifiably refuse to accommodate a guest, or to eject a guest who has already been received. Some of the qualifications are unexceptionable but others are open to debate. As McDonald has observed[98]:

> "... a note of caution. Whilst the wide terms in which the principles might be expressed might not change, social and

---

98 M McDonald, 'A commentary on the Hotel Proprietors Act 1963', *unpublished conference paper, 1987.*

economic circumstances do. What was considered an unreasonable refusal twenty years ago might not be thought so now and vice versa."

This is particularly so given that many of the authorities stretch back to the 19th century and beyond, when prevailing social attitudes were much different and economic conditions were different too.

The guest must be a traveller

Originally it was a requirement that to demand entry the guest had to be a traveller i.e. a passenger or wayfarer not a neighbour or friend.[99] As one commentator has explained:

"There are compelling reasons why the keeper of a hotel should be forced to give lodging and food to a weary traveler, away from home, and in dire need of rest and refreshment, but none why others should be so favored."[100]

However we have seen that this is no longer the case.[101] There is now no requirement in English law that a guest must have travelled any distance at all. The definition of traveller is now so wide as to encompass anyone who comes to the hotel for the purposes of eating, drinking or being accommodated.[102]

Although the guest need not show that he is a traveller when he arrives, nevertheless a change of status from guest to lodger will deprive him of his rights as a guest. In the words of Lord Anderson in *Rothfield*:

"No one can successfully claim to make his home in an inn, and an innkeeper is not bound to provide residence to anyone."

---

99   *Calye's Case 8 Co Rep 32a; 77 ER 520. R v Lluellin 12 Mod 446; 88 ER 1441*

100 *'Innkeepers Right to Exclude or Eject Guests' 7 Fordham Law Review 417 (1938)*

101 *See Chapter 2*

102 *Williams v Linnitt [1951] 1 KB 565*

This was the issue at the heart of the case of *Lamond v Richard and the Gordon Hotels Ltd.*[103] In that case a woman had been received at an hotel in the capacity of guest and had then resided there for ten months. After this period of time the hotelkeeper ejected her. It was held by the Court of Appeal that on the facts she had ceased to be a guest and had become a lodger and therefore could be lawfully ejected. Whether she was a traveller or a lodger was a question of fact and mere length of residence was not decisive but it was certainly one of the factors which must be taken into account in determining the character of her stay.

No room

The leading case here is *Browne v Brandt.*[104] In that case the claimant was travelling by car from Crawley to London but late at night broke down on the way and had to walk. He reached The Chequers at about two o'clock in the morning and demanded a bed for himself and a friend who was travelling with him. The defendant refused, saying that the hotel was full. The claimant then demanded refreshment and after some discussion the defendant admitted them and served them refreshments. Subsequently the claimant indicated to the defendant that he and his companion would be happy to spend the night in the coffee room but the defendant refused. In an action in the County Court for breach of the common law duty to accommodate travellers the judge found that all six bedrooms at the hotel were full on the night in question and that the hotelkeeper was not bound to accommodate the claimant in either the coffee room or the lounge. The claimant appealed but the appellate court came to a similar conclusion:

> "I cannot think that the authorities to which we have been referred shew that where an innkeeper provides a certain number of bedrooms and sitting-rooms for the accommodation of guests he is under a legal obligation to

103 *[1897] 1 QB 541*
104 *[1902] 1 KB 696*

receive and shelter as many people as can be put into the rooms without over-crowding. I think a person who comes to the inn has no legal right to demand to pass the night in a public sitting-room if the bedrooms are all full, and I think that the landlord has no obligation to receive him. The landlord must act reasonably; he must not captiously or unreasonably refuse to receive persons when he has proper accommodation for them. Here the county court judge has found, in effect, that the defendant did act reasonably." (Lord Alverstone CJ)

Of much more interest however are the words of Darling J who addressed the issue of what is meant by 'full' and how this concept may have changed over the years:

"The question then arises, when an innkeeper's house may properly be said to be full. I do not think that the old cases can help one very much, because in olden times people were in the habit of sleeping many in one room, and several in one bed. People who were absolutely unknown to each other would sleep in the same room, as is done in common lodging-houses at the present time. Therefore, if we got a definition of "full" in one of the old cases, I should not be surprised to find among that what was called "full" then we should now call "indecent overcrowding". It is the habit now of people to occupy separate bedrooms, and, having regard to the ordinary way of living at the present time, I think an inn may be said to be full for the purpose of affording accommodation for the night if all the bedrooms are occupied. There might have been a difficulty here if the plaintiff had said, "I will take your sitting-room. I do not want to go to bed. I will sit up all night." But that difficulty does not arise on the facts of this case. The county court judge has found that the house was full having regard to modern ways of living. He referred to Chaucer and the Canterbury pilgrims. One need look only at the "Sentimental Journey" to see how people's habits have altered since the time of Laurence Sterne."[105]

A fit state

Many of the authorities as well as the Hotel Proprietors Act declare that the traveller must be in a fit state if he wishes to assert his right to be received. The phrase covers a multitude of sins. At one end of the scale there are cases which state that a traveller can be turned away for violent and drunken behaviour while at the other end there are cases where the hotelkeeper has refused travellers simply for the way they are dressed or because of their character. Between these extremes are a range of cases involving travellers with vicious dogs or unacceptable luggage. According to Sherry:[106]

> "the improper conduct or objectionable character or condition of a guest or prospective guest will generally be held to be grounds for refusal to admit. This is so partially because an innkeeper has a duty to all of his guests to protect their persons and property and therefore must be able to exclude persons who are likely to injure or disturb other guests. Also, the public interest which the law seeks to protect in imposing a duty to receive all guests would hardly be served by requiring the innkeeper to receive and accommodate undesirables."

He concedes however that what amounts to objectionable character or condition or improper conduct is not easily defined. Ultimately the test is one of reasonableness.

An American case involving the ejection of a prostitute, *Raider v Dixie Inn*,[107] gives a flavour of the scope of this exception:

---

105 *For a contemporary account of the kind of overcrowding that existed in the late 17th century see 'The Illustrated Journeys of Celia Fiennes 1685–1712', p.108, ed. Christopher Morris, MacDonald, 1982.*

106 *'The Laws of Innkeepers', 3rd ed., 1993, Cornell*

107 *198 Ky 152, 248 SW 229 (1923)*

It appears, therefore, fully settled that an innkeeper may lawfully refuse to entertain objectionable characters, if to do so is calculated to injure his business or to place himself, business, or guests in a hazardous, uncomfortable, or dangerous situation. The innkeeper need not accept anyone as a guest who is calculated to and will injure his business. A prizefighter who has been guilty of law breaking may be excluded. *Nelson v Boldt*, 180 F 779 [ED Pa 1910]. Neither is an innkeeper required to entertain a card sharp, *Watkins v Cope*, 84 NJL 143, 86 A 545 [1913]; a thief, *Markham v Brown*, 8 NH 523 [1837]; persons of bad reputation or those who are under suspicion, *Goodenow v Travis*, 3 Johns (NY) 427 [Sup Ct 1808]; drunken and disorderly persons, *Atwater v Sawyer*, 76 Me 539 [1884]; one who commits a trespass by breaking in the door, *Goodenow v Travis, supra*; one who is filthy or who subjects the guests to annoyance, *Pidgeon v Legge*, 5 Week Rep 649, [21 JP 743 (Ex 1857)].

Before examining the caselaw in any detail it is necessary to mention that underpinning the traveller's right to be received at common law there is now extensive statutory protection available to the traveller who is discriminated against on the grounds of race, sex or disability.[108] These statutory provisions will be examined in the next chapter.

Drunkenness

The hotelkeeper does not have to accept a traveller in an inebriated state. The case of *Hawthorn v Hammond*[109] provides an illustration. The facts of the case were that the plaintiff and his brother arrived at the Wheel Inn at Worfield on the road between Bridgnorth and Kidderminster between 9 and 10 o'clock at night. The inn was shut up

---

108 *Sex Discrimination Act 1975; Race Relations Act 1976; Disability Discrimination Act 1995*

109 *174 ER 866 (1844)*

but the plaintiff's brother got out of their gig and knocked with his fist and kicked on the door for over 10 minutes but was unable to obtain admission. They went away but returned later and knocked again but were still not admitted. The plaintiff sued the innkeeper for refusing to receive them. In his summing up to the jury Park B said:

> "... you will therefore have to say whether you were satisfied that the noise made by the plaintiff's brother was really heard by the defendant; and if so, whether you think that she thought to have concluded from it that the persons so knocking at the door were persons requiring to be admitted as guests, or whether she might have concluded that they were drunken persons, who had come there to make a disturbance."

And in the case of *R v Ivens*[110] Coleridge J said:

> "If a person came to an inn drunk, or behaved in an indecent or improper manner, I am of opinion that the innkeeper is not bound to receive him."

But even drunkenness is a matter of degree. Would it be reasonable to turn away a traveller who was only slightly tipsy or a little the worse for wear but not violent or abusive? Given that many hotels offer not only accommodation but also restaurants and bars it would be curious indeed if a traveller were turned away for having had a couple of drinks if the hotel was happy to receive a sober traveller and then permit him to drink as much as he liked in the hotel bar or from the mini-bar in his room. In reality, given modern society's tolerance of alcohol consumption, this is highly unlikely to happen, and if it does, the refusal on grounds of drunkenness may merely disguise a refusal for other, unacceptable, reasons such as race discrimination or simply on grounds of personal whim.

---

110 *7 C & P 213 (1835)*

Clothing

There are two widely quoted cases on this issue, *Pidgeon v Legge*[111] and *R v Sprague*[112] The first case is relatively straightforward. The plaintiff was a chimney sweep who went into a bar in his working clothes. The landlord requested him to go and change his clothes but the plaintiff refused. The landlord then called the police to remove him from the bar and in the ensuing struggle the plaintiff's leg was broken. On appeal to the Court of Exchequer it was held that as the plaintiff was in an unfit condition the landlord was justified in ordering his removal. Bramwell B said:

> "In the first place, the defendant's house was, I think, not an inn; and in the second place, if it were, but the plaintiff being in an unfit condition to be there, the defendant was justified in insisting upon his leaving."

The second case is much more difficult. The defendant, Mrs Sprague, had been indicted for refusing to serve food to Lady Harberton. Lady Harberton was a member of the Cyclists' Touring Club and she invariably wore 'rational costume',[113] a form of clothing resembling bloomers worn by radical Victorian women, when she went cycling. On the occasion in question she had stopped at the Hautboy Hotel and said that she would like lunch. Mrs Sprague had refused to serve her in the coffee room on account of her dress but said that she would be prepared to serve lunch either in a private room, which would cost extra, or in the bar parlour at the back of the hotel. There was a conflict of evidence about the state of this room. According to Lady Harberton there were men smoking in the room and the smell was abominable. The defendant on the other hand said that the room was frequently used by both ladies and gentlemen for lunch and there were

---

111 *21 JP 743 (1857)*

112 *63 JP 233 (1899)*

113 *'The Move Towards Rational dress', Margie Knauff, www.mpmbooks.com/amelia/RATIONAL.HTM; 'The Debate Over Women's Clothing: 'Rational' or Ladylike dress', Justina Rodrigues, http://nadal.loynoledu/history/journal/1989-0/rodrigues.htm*

always flowers there. Lady Harberton took this offer of what she considered to be an unsuitable room as a refusal to serve her and left the hotel. Subsequently the Cyclists Touring Club took it upon themselves to prosecute Mrs Sprague in a test case.

The report of the case gives this account of the Chairman of the Magistrates' summing up to the jury:

> "... an innkeeper could not refuse to supply a traveller with food and lodging without some lawful excuse. Here Mrs Sprague did not say that she had a right to dictate to Lady Harberton what dress she was to wear. Therefore the question whether ladies should or should not wear rational dress was not in dispute. An innkeeper could not refuse to supply food because of the particular shape of the dress of the traveller. The only question, therefore, was whether there was a refusal to supply food in a decent and proper place. The innkeeper could select the room provided it was a decent and proper room. Nor, in his opinion, was a guest entitled to have a room exactly to his or her taste. The jury must judge by the requirements of ordinary and reasonable persons. The learned Chairman then referred to the evidence, and asked the jury to consider whether the bar parlour was a decent and proper room for a guest to have lunch in; and, further, whether the bar parlour was not to all intents and purposes part of the hotel."

The jury returned a verdict of not guilty, presumably on the basis that the alternative offered was a decent and proper room. Given that Mrs Sprague admitted in evidence that she always refused to serve women in rational costume in the coffee room it would be interesting to speculate what the verdict would have been if the bar parlour had been unsuitable or if indeed the hotel had had no alternatives to offer. In those circumstances, according to the chairman, Mrs Sprague would have had no alternative but to have entertained Lady Harberton in the coffee room.

Sherry comments that it is inconceivable that a case such as *Sprague* would arise today. Imagine, he says, the Hilton Hawaiian Village objecting to a woman wearing a bikini. He qualifies this however by saying that the management might be justified in refusing to permit such attire being worn in the main dining room.[114]

The issue of dress codes has been explored by McDonald writing in 1991 from an Irish perspective.[115] He describes the position in Ireland, where the law is substantially the same as in England, in the following terms:

> "Many hotels in Ireland, and especially higher grade and Dublin hotels, tend to enforce dress codes on their customers, with the result that they quite frequently refuse to admit customers who do not conform with their code. In the higher grade and Dublin hotels, the dress code tends to apply throughout the entire hotel, and is therefore enforced at the point of entry into the hotel, whereas in rural hotels that have dress codes the code is often applied to just one area inside the hotel – the restaurant. The ostensible reason for the dress code is that the hotel does not want customers on the premises whose outward dress and appearance does not conform to the maintenance or improvement of the ambiance of the hotel, as set by a combination of the standard of dress and appearance of the existing clientele's socio-economic grouping and the hotel's own efforts to create an ambiance appropriate to the type of customer it wishes to attract."

Whether a breach of the dress code justifies a refusal is a question of reasonableness. However he rightly points out that such refusals are often:

> "... a facade to enable the hotel to refuse admittance to 'undesirables". In other words, and to borrow a concept

---

114 P.144

115 'Admission and Refusal Law in Hotels – The Appearance of Customers', *Gazette of the Incorporated Law Society of Ireland, p.177, June 1991.*

from sex discrimination law – whether the operation of the code amounts to indirect social discrimination against a particular segment of the population by setting standards of dress which are not absolutely essential to the successful running of the hotel and which a significantly greater proportion of one social group can comply with than another. If the dress code causes indirect social discrimination, then it is almost certainly in breach of s.3(1) of the Hotel Proprietors Act 1963, because its use to achieve an unstated and masked indirect effect is, by definition, unreasonable"

To test the reasonableness of the refusal he suggests that the following factors should be taken into account:

- The individual items of clothing, or style of clothing, or footwear of prospective customers.

- The degree to which a hotel is allowed to pick its own ambiance given the definition of a hotel in s.1(1) [of the Hotel Proprietors Act 1963] that it provide for "all-comers".

- The finding of a rational relationship, or linkage, between the item of clothing and the operation or ambiance of the hotel.

- The degree to which different social groupings tend to wear such items, or styles, of clothing.

- Whether the hotel code is operated in an even-handed and consistent manner and whether facilities are made available by the hotel to enable non-complying customers to comply with the dress code.

It may also be relevant to the reasonableness of the refusal to look at the circumstances in which the guest presents him or herself and what services they require. Take the following example. My car breaks down in a remote part of Northumberland, late at night in the middle of a storm and I am unable to summon help with my mobile phone. I set out to look for help wearing only my faded jeans, an old T-shirt, and an old coat. By the time that I arrive at the nearest settlement, having stumbled and fallen several times, I am not only wet through but also muddy and bloodied. I present myself at the hotel in the village – an exclusive country house hotel. Can they refuse to take me in on the grounds that I am inappropriately dressed? We would venture to say no. Such a refusal would surely undercut the whole rationale on which the hotelkeeper's obligations are based – the obligation to take in needy travellers. Should the ambiance and exclusivity of their establishment be permitted to override my need for food and shelter? Surely not.

On the other hand what if I turn up at the same hotel in the middle of the day, similarly attired and equally wet, but only requiring lunch while the garage in the village repairs my car? I may not want a bed but I am very hungry and tired and in need of something to eat and drink. Are they justified in turning me away from their Michelin three star restaurant? If, as in *Sprague*, the hotelkeeper can offer a suitable alternative, such as a bar, then they can direct me there and the refusal is reasonable, or as in *Pidgeon v Legge*, my clothes are so wet and dirty they are likely to damage the property then a refusal may be justified. However if there is only one restaurant and my clothes are only inappropriate rather than likely to do harm the answer is much more difficult.

In practical terms I may not present myself in such a state because I would be intimidated or embarrassed, or the hotelkeeper might avoid the problem by claiming that all the tables had been reserved, but that is to evade the question rather than answer it. What it comes down to is that an ancient and important principle of the common law finds itself at odds with modern commercial practice and accepted social norms. The question is, which should take precedence. Our answer is that the presumption in favour of the obligation to receive all comers should be such as to prevail except in the most extreme circumstances and should certainly override any temporary embarrassment to the hotelkeeper that might occur in the examples given above.

Character

Although an hotelkeeper cannot pick and choose his guests he does have a discretion to refuse entry to persons of bad character or reputation. *Rothfield v North British Railway Co* provides a prime example of this principle. In *Rothfield* the court referred with approval to the case of *Strathearn Hydropathic Company v Inland Revenue*[116] in which it was said that the law allows:

> "... a pretty wide discretion in hotelkeepers as to rejecting guests that are not suitable."[117]

In *Rothfield* itself the court pushed the boundaries of that discretion to its very limits and probably beyond when they upheld the right of the hotelkeeper to reject a Jewish money-lender. The facts of the case, as found by Lord Salvesen were as follows:

> "Summarising that evidence it comes to this; that the pursuer, who is a Jew by religion and of alien extraction, bearing a thinly disguised Teutonic name, and practising the unpopular profession of a money-lender, had made himself somewhat conspicuous at the hotel by his swaggering conduct and had been the subject of remark by other guests; that, at the time when the country was still at war, and the hotel was largely frequented by young naval and military officers, he associated a great deal with such officers and entertained several on more than one occasion; that the directors came to the bona fide conclusion that he was using the hotel and associating with these young men for business purposes, and that his presence at the hotel was objected to by other guests. Added to all this the pursuer had the misfortune of being associated in business with another Jewish money-lender named Cohen, who, in November 1917, was convicted of a fraudulent conspiracy in connexion with recruiting, and

---

116 *(1881) 8 R 798*
117 *Lord Justice-Clerk at p.827.*

received a sentence of eight months' imprisonment. In the same article in 'Truth' in which these facts were published, the pursuer himself was exposed as a money-lender who had bled one of his victims "in the most rapacious way". The full details of the transactions on which this charge was based were published, and the pursuer has taken no means to vindicate his character. The attack made in the public press upon the pursuer was brought to the directors' knowledge, and it was only then that they finally made up their minds to take definite action."

In the same case Lord Ormidale found:

"He [Rothfield] had become notorious and an object of suspicion and offence to the other guests, and according to the best judgment the directors could form he was endeavouring to use their premises for operating his business. It would not be reasonable, it seems to me, to exact from them absolute proof that their suspicions were well-founded. It is enough that it clearly appears that they had reasonable grounds for thinking as they did, and, that they did not act rashly or capriciously, but on the contrary came to an honest conclusion only after patient and anxious consideration of the whole circumstances. On this evidence I think that their contention that they were justified in refusing to receive the pursuer into their hotel is well-founded."

There seem to be at least three elements forming the basis of the judgment. First, that the pursuer, Rothfield, was a Jew and a money-lender. Although these factors can clearly be seen to be colouring their view of the pursuer there is no statement, nor would one expect to find one, that he could be excluded simply because he was a Jew or a money-lender. The only statements on these matters are that they do *not* give rise to a right to reject. As such the judgment is unexceptional.

The second element of the decision is whether or not Rothfield was actually conducting a money-lending business on the premises of the hotel. If so, this was clearly an illegal act and he could have been excluded for that. The problem however was that there was no direct proof that he was conducting his business in the hotel. The view of the court, expressed in the extracts above from the judgments of Lords Salvesen and Ormidale, was that the evidence given by the two directors of the hotel gave rise to a reasonable suspicion and that was sufficient. There was however an opinion by Lord Anderson in the court below which differed on the inference to be drawn from the evidence. He concluded that the evidence was not strong enough to support a reasonable suspicion:

> "The question, then, comes to be whether the defenders have proved that the pursuer either conducted money-lending business in the hotel, or attempted to do so. Were the suspicions of Mr Gray and Mr Younger [The Directors of the North British Hotel] well-founded? I am unable to hold that they were. It was certainly not a necessary inference from what they saw to conclude that the pursuer was trying to prosecute his business. I do not think the inference was even justifiable or reasonable. The pursuer had relatives in the army, one of whom gave evidence on his behalf, and his motives in entertaining and conversing with British officers were probably entirely different from those suggested. No officer has been brought to prove that the directors' suspicions were well-founded. I quite appreciate the defenders' difficulty in obtaining such evidence; but it is for them to prove this part of the case and the conclusion I reach is that they have failed to do so."

It is of course always possible to differ on questions of fact but the differing interpretations do not reveal any irreconcilable differences as to the law. The conclusion arrived at by all the judges involved in the case was that if there is a reasonable suspicion of conduct which would give rise to a right to reject then that is sufficient justification.

The third element, and the most controversial, is that he was a disagreeable person whom the other guests found offensive. The problem here is where to draw the line. Have we not all been in hotels where for one reason or another we have been offended by other guests, whether it be the way they dress or their opinionated views or their politics or their profession? But this is no reason to have someone excluded. If an hotelkeeper were allowed to exclude such persons simply because they wished to pander to the prejudices of their existing clientele then this would effectively drive a coach and horses through the right to be received. It may be uncomfortable for the other guests and it may even be unprofitable for the hotelkeeper but that is no reason to succumb to bigotry, intolerance or racism. Significantly, the court in *Constantine* was not prepared to support the management of the Imperial Hotel when it yielded to the prejudices of its American clientele who objected to the presence of a black man in the hotel.

The problem with *Rothfield* however is that the tenor of the judgments leaves one with more than a suspicion that the court's disapproval of his religion and occupation, when coupled with his swaggering personality, spilled over into their assessment of whether there were reasonable grounds for believing he was conducting an illegal business on the premises.

But this is not to say that there may not come a point where the character, reputation and demeanour of the potential guest is such that the offence taken by other guests is legitimate, thus justifying a rejection by the hotelkeeper. The following passage taken from an article written in 1938, comments not only on the *Rothfield* decision, but is also not afraid to venture an opinion as to where the author would draw the line:[118]

> "The court justified the innkeeper on the grounds that the presence of such a person at the hotel would have been disagreeable to the other patrons and prejudicial to the house. This test is unsound. Neither loss of patronage, nor mere "disagreeableness" to the other guests, has ever been

---

118 *'Innkeepers Right to Exclude or Reject Guests' 7 Fordham Law Review 417, (1938)*

sufficient to justify exclusion. However, under such a rule it would be permissable to deny entrance to a gangster whose notorious affiliations with corruption would make him unwelcome in decent society.

In defining the character and reputation that warrant rejection at a hotel, it will be helpful, because of the analogous liabilities of these occupations, to note the corresponding right which justifies a carrier in refusing to transport a traveler. It is held that the private character of the traveler is no concern of the carrier, unless it will affect his conduct on the train. No matter how infamous a person is, if his public demeanor is respectable, he must be given transport. Thus, a known prostitute cannot be denied carriage when her behavior in public is unimpeachable. Such a rule can well be incorporated into the law of hotels. True, an innkeeper may keep out one who would bring discomfort to his guests. But the presence of a person, known to be privately immoral, yet acting decorously, can disturb only the fastidious, and the necessities of the traveling public must be protected before these nice sensibilities. It is submitted that the presence of a bad character brings no direct physical discomfort, but offends only the moral sense. An advocate of euthanasia would hardly be less offensive, yet who would deny his right to accommodation at a hotel? Private virtue cannot be made a condition precedent to admission. But the inveterate thief, who probably will purloin the goods of host and fellow guests can rightfully be denied admission; similarly, a woman of such immoral nature that misconduct in the hotel is reasonably expected, cannot complain if refused accommodation. Obviously, one who intends objectionable conduct forfeits his right to enter."

We said earlier that the court in *Rothfield* cited with approval the dictum in the *Strathearn* case that the hotelkeeper had a 'pretty wide discretion' when it came to rejecting potential guests. Quite how far the court in Strathearn would have been prepared to go is illustrated by the following passage:

> "He [the hotelkeeper] is bound also, I think, to exercise a discretion as to the class of people whom he will admit to his hotel. A man who is carrying on business as a hotelkeeper in a first-class establishment is not bound to admit to his hotel persons in every rank and condition of life. Sometimes persons in the condition of working men become, for the time, very rich and extravagant. We have heard tales of navvies drinking up all the champagne, and eating all the spring chickens of a whole neighbourhood; and if any of that class of people presented themselves to a hotelkeeper of the character we are supposing, I cannot doubt that he would have a discretion to reject them, because their manners and habits are not suitable to the class of people whom he receives."

Such attitudes are unlikely to strike a judicial chord in today's less class-dominated society but they are illustrative of McDonald's warning, quoted earlier, that social and economic circumstances change, and with them what might be regarded as a reasonable refusal.

Illness

There is a dearth of authority on the circumstances in which a guest can be rejected or ejected on grounds of illness. *R v Luellin*[119] is cited regularly but is of dubious value. The whole report consists of the following passage:

> "Indictment against an innkeeper for not receiving a sick person must state he was a traveller.
>
> The defendant was master of the Bell Inn, in Bristol. He was indicted for not receiving one taken ill with the smallpox; and it was quashed, for not saying he was a traveller."

119 *88 ER 1441 (1701)*

The decision therefore is not that the refusal was reasonable but simply that the case was not pleaded properly. Despite this lack of clarity it would nevertheless seem reasonable to refuse a guest with a serious contagious or notifiable disease, simply on the grounds that this would be necessary to protect other guests.

As for guests who have already been received the position is summed up by Sherry:[120]

> "If a guest at the inn becomes ill, it is the duty of the innkeeper to treat him with the consideration due to a sick person. In the discharge of his duty, the innkeeper may call a physician to examine the guest, and if so requested by the guest, to treat him. Many hotels keep a doctor on call for such contingencies. If the guest refuses treatment or medical services and if, in the opinion of the physician who examined him, the guest's condition is serious, the guest may be removed to a hospital. In the event the diagnosis is one of a contagious disease, the guest must be moved to a hospital promptly and under medical supervision to protect the other guests in the house and to preserve public health.
>
> Of primary importance in dealing with an ill guest is caution and consideration for the guest's condition."

Inability to pay

The right to refuse extends to those who cannot pay a reasonable price for the accommodation or who will not tender payment when requested:

> "An hotel-keeper is not bound to receive a guest until the price of the accommodation is tendered. He is not obliged to accommodate a guest on trust. He may eject a guest for proper cause. Where after the admission of a guest circumstances arise which, had they existed when he

---

120 *P.148*

applied for admission, would have justified the hotel-keeper in refusing to admit him, they will justify the hotel-keeper in ejecting him. Just as the hotel-keeper may refuse to admit a traveller unless he pay in advance, so he may eject him if after admission he fails on demand to pay the amount due the hotel-keeper." MacDonald DCJ, *Bellairs v Yale Hotel Calgary Ltd* [1936] 1 WWR 316 (Can).

The corollary of this is that the hotelkeeper can only charge a reasonable sum. He may not charge what he chooses for otherwise he may exclude anyone, however indiscriminately, simply by arbitrarily setting the price too high.

> "They [travellers] do not deal upon contracts as others do, they only make bills, in which they cannot set unreasonable rates; if they do, they are indictable for extortion ..." (*Newton v Trigg* 89 ER 566 (1691))

What amounts to a reasonable sum is debatable but in *Rothfield* the court described what the usual position will be:

> "In the ordinary case, however, a guest entering the hotel does so on the footing that the usual tariff charges will be made. These charges are revised from time to time, in accordance with the rise and fall of prices, but at any given time they are fixed."

The position is not much different today. Hotels are obliged by law[121] to display their rack rate, which they may vary of course from time to time, but which they cannot arbitrarily raise simply in order to refuse someone whom they would otherwise have to accommodate.

Nature of Guest's Property

The duty of the hotelkeeper to receive all comers extends to their luggage as well. In *Robins & Co v Gray*[122] Lord Esher MR said:

---

121 *Tourism (Sleeping Accommodation Price Display) Order 1977.* SI 1977 No. 1877

122 *[1895] 2 QB 501*

"If a traveller comes to an inn with goods which are his luggage – I do not say his personal luggage, but his luggage – the innkeeper by the law of the land is bound to take him and his luggage in. The innkeeper cannot discriminate and say that he will take in the traveller but not his luggage. If the traveller brought something exceptional which is not luggage – such as a tiger or a package of dynamite – the innkeeper might refuse to take it in; but the custom of the realm is that, unless there is some reason to the contrary in the exceptional character of the things brought, he must take in the traveller and his goods."

In *R v Rymer*[123] the court held that it would be reasonable to refuse a guest who brought dogs with him that other guests found objectionable – their number, their behaviour, their size and their kind.

Offer of Alternative Accommodation

In both *Constantine* and *Rothfield* the issue was raised of whether the fact that alternative accommodation was available made any difference. In both cases the court answered no. In the lower court in *Rothfield* Lord Anderson said:

"It was suggested that, as the pursuer might have obtained accommodation at another hotel in Edinburgh, he was not entitled to insist on obtaining it at the defenders' hotel. I do not agree. A traveller is, in my opinion, entitled to choose the hotel at which he desires to be a guest, and the defenders are not entitled to put a traveller, desiring to use their hotel, to the trouble and expense of finding another hotel."

In *Constantine*, when the plaintiff had been refused accommodation at the Imperial Hotel, he was offered alternative accommodation at the defendant's other hotel, the Bedford. The defendants endeavoured to make out that there had been no refusal by them – on the grounds that he had in fact been accommodated by them, albeit at another hotel

---

123 *(1877) 2 QBD 136*

---

altogether. In rejecting this submission Birkett J approved the passage above and went on to say:

> "The claim before me is that the defendants refused to receive and lodge Mr Constantine at the Imperial Hotel, and I hold it to be no answer that Mr Constantine went to the Bedford Hotel under protest."

CHAPTER FOUR

HOTELS AND DISCRIMINATION LAW. THE RITZ, LIKE THE LAW, IS OPEN TO EVERYONE

Introduction

In the UK and other common law jurisdictions such as the US, Australia and Canada, we have seen in Chapter Three that a traveller has a legal right to be received by a hotelkeeper and can only be refused for very limited reasons. This common law right has been bolstered in recent years by a raft of legislation aimed at preventing discrimination on grounds of sex,[124] race[125] and, most recently, disability.[126] All the legislation is of general application but clearly embraces accommodation suppliers such as hotelkeepers within its ambit. We shall start by examining the disability discrimination legislation and then go on to discuss sex and race discrimination. In that it imposes duties on hotelkeepers to take positive measures to accommodate disabled guests, the Disability Discrimination Act 1995 (DDA) goes further than the other legislation, which probably added little to a guest's common law right to be accommodated.

Disability Discrimination

It is beyond the scope of this book to examine the rationale behind the DDA except in the very broadest terms. Suffice it to say that in the early 1990's, prior to the passage of the Act, pressure on the Government compelled it to recognise the phenomenon of disability discrimination and to concede that there was social exclusion and marginalisation of a sizeable minority. It is probably a rationalisation

124 *Sex Discrimination Act 1975*
125 *Race Relations Act 1976*
126 *Disability Discrimination Act 1995*

rather than a rationale, but as the Government has pointed out,[127] there are some 8.5 million disabled people in the UK and a recent estimate put their collective spending power at over £40bn a year. One in four customers is disabled or is close to someone who is. Accessible services are attractive services. Changes which help people with disabilities also make services more convenient for everyone to use. There may well be financial advantages to be gained because adjustments for disabled people may also benefit other customers, such as those with baby buggies, enabling service providers to improve their overall level of service and attract more customers.

The Scope of the Legislation

The Act aims to protect 'disabled persons' who suffer 'discrimination' in

● employment,

● access to goods or services,

● relation to premises, or

● relation to public transport.

We are concerned here only with the provisions relating to access to goods and services to be found in Part III of the Act.

The scheme of the Act is to create a legislative framework of primary duties which are supplemented by subordinate legislation in the form of statutory instruments and by codes of practice. There have been four codes of practice issued under the act,[128] the current one being the 'Disability Discrimination Act Code of Practice – Rights of Access: services to the public, public authority functions, private clubs and premises', which came into effect in December 2006.[129] All of the Codes have had suggestions which relate specifically to the hotel and catering sector. The status of the Code is rather like the Highway Code; it does not impose legal obligations nor is it an authoritative

---

127 *Disability Rights Commission 2000. Overcoming physical barriers to access for disabled customers: a practical guide for smaller service providers*

128 *The three previous ones being issued in 1996, 1999 and 2002.*

129 *ISBN 0117036951*

statement of the law. However under the Act it can be used in proceedings under the DDA and any provision which appears to the court to be relevant must be taken into account.[130]

One distinctive feature of the legislation is the duty imposed on service providers to make reasonable adjustments to enable disabled persons to obtain access to goods and services. This duty is broken down into three elements –

● the duty to make adjustments to policies, practices and procedures,[131]

● the duty to provide auxiliary aids,[132] and

● the duty to make adjustments to physical features.[133]

All three duties were brought into effect by 2004. The policy reasons underpinning these provisions were acknowledged in the 1994 Green Paper which stated that:

> "... removing physical impediments does nothing to banish the mental barriers of ignorance and prejudice. Making buildings easier to get into is of no avail if disabled people are kept outside because their appearance or behaviour is deemed too upsetting for other patrons or through misguided concerns for their safety"[134]

Who has rights under the Act?

By virtue of s.1(2) of the Act a disabled person is defined as a person with a 'disability' – which is defined in s.1(1) in the following fashion:

> "... a person has a disability ... if he has a physical or mental impairment which has a substantial and long-term effect on his ability to carry out normal day-to-day activities."

---

130 DDA s.53

131 S.21(1) DDA 1995

132 S.21(4) DDA

133 S.21(2) DDA 1995

134 *A Consultation on Government Measures to Tackle Discrimination Against Disabled People (July 1994) para 4.2 (the 'Green Paper')*

Physical or mental impairment includes sensory impairments. Hidden impairments are also covered (for example, mental illness or mental health problems, learning disabilities and conditions such as diabetes or epilepsy). People who have had a disability in the past are protected from discrimination even if they no longer have the disability.[135]

Part III of the Act only addresses discrimination to disabled persons as consumers themselves. Members of a family who are refused accommodation in a hotel because they are accompanied by a child with disabilities have no remedy *under the Act*. Of course under this scenario the child will have been discriminated against and will have a cause of action.

Upon whom is the duty imposed?

The duty not to discriminate is imposed upon 'service providers'. This term is defined in s.19(2)(b) as being a person who 'is concerned with the provision, in the United Kingdom, of services to the public or to a section of the public.' Section 19 further states that the provision of services includes the provision of *any* goods or facilities and that it is irrelevant whether the service is provided for payment or not.

Section 19(3) provides a non-exhaustive list of examples of services to which the legislation applies. These illustrations include a number which may be relevant to the hospitality industry:

● access to and use of any place which members of the public are permitted to enter

● access to and use of means of communication

● access to and use of information services

● accommodation in a hotel, boarding house or other similar establishment

● facilities for entertainment, recreation or refreshment

Liability falls not only upon the service provider but also upon employees, contractors and agents.[136]

---

135 *DDA s.2(1)*
136 *DDA s.57*

A service might appear to be provided by more than one service provider. In such a case it may be important to identify who is actually responsible for the provision of the service which has given rise to the alleged discrimination. In some cases liability under the Act may be shared among a number of service providers.

The 2006 Code provides the following example:

"A training company provides a non-residential conference at a hotel. The training company is responsible for any duties that may arise under the Act in respect of the conduct of the conference and the choice of an accessible venue. However, the hotel may provide some services that are part of the conference facilities, such as toilets, for which it is responsible under the Act. In addition, services provided by the hotel that are ancillary to the conference (for example, accommodation the night before the conference) are also those for which the hotel is likely to be liable under the Act."[137]

Services not available to the public, such as those provided by private clubs, were not originally covered by Part III of the Act. This has now changed and there are extensive provisions relating to private clubs.

Private clubs are generally those where membership is a condition of participation and members have to comply with a genuine process of selection, usually by a club committee operating the club rules. However simply calling a service a "club" does not necessarily mean that the courts will consider it to be a private club.

A health club in a hotel is open to the public. Club members pay an annual subscription and are provided with a membership card. Before using the club's fitness equipment, a member must undergo a fitness test. Although members have to satisfy certain requirements in order to use some of the facilities, compliance with a genuine selection procedure for membership is not a

---

137 *Para. 10.17*

condition of using the club. The club is providing services to the public and is likely to be covered by the provisions relating to services to the public.[138]

Meaning of Discrimination

Sections 19–21 provide a complex definition of what amounts to unlawful discrimination. Broadly speaking the legislation provides as follows:

- Section 19 makes it unlawful for a provider of services to discriminate against a disabled person in a number of specified ways in relation to the provision of goods, facilities or services

- Section 21 places a duty on service providers to make reasonable adjustments to enable disabled persons to obtain access to the services

- Section 20 defines discrimination as treating a disabled person less favourably or by failing to comply with the duty to make reasonable adjustments without justification

We will look at each element of this definition in turn bearing in mind that they are clearly interdependent and that to see them in isolation may give an incomplete view initially.

The general duty not to discriminate unlawfully – section 19.

Section 19 makes it unlawful for a service provider to discriminate against a disabled person:

- In refusing to provide or deliberately not providing a service which he provides to the public (s.19(1)(a))

- In failing to comply with a duty to make reasonable adjustments under s.21 with the effect that it is impossible or unreasonably difficult for a disabled person to make use of any service (s.19(1)(b))

- In the standard of service provided to disabled persons or the manner in which the service is provided (s.19(1)(c))

- In the terms on which the service is provided to disabled persons (s.19(1)(d))

---

138 *Code of Practice. Para. 3.11*

The first instance is simply a straightforward case of direct discrimination. If the hotel simply adopts a policy of not accepting reservations from disabled persons that would fall into this category. For example if they refused to accommodate a person with cerebral palsy because of that individual's disability they would be committing an unlawful act of discrimination. The 2002 Code of Practice gave the following illustration:

> "A disabled person with Tourette's syndrome (which causes him to utter obscenities involuntarily and compulsively) wishes to book a hotel room. The hotel receptionist pretends that all rooms are taken in order to refuse his booking because of his disability This is likely to be against the law."[139]

The second we will come to later when we look at the requirement to make reasonable adjustments. The third would cover cases where for instance an hotel, in order to dissuade disabled guests from staying adopted a policy of making them wait at check-in, of not offering them suitable rooms, of not seating or serving them promptly in the restaurant, of not passing on messages, of not cleaning the rooms as regularly as for able bodied guests, etc. The fourth would apply where disabled guests were simply charged more for the provision of the same services as able-bodied guests.

The definition of discrimination – section 20

Section 20 provides that

(1) For the purposes of section 19 a provider of services discriminates against a disabled person if–

(a) for a reason which relates to the disabled person's disability, he treats him less favourably than he treats or would treat others to whom that reason does not or would not apply; and

---

139 *Para. 3.14, Code of Practice*

(b) he cannot show that the less favourable treatment in question is justified.

(2) For the purposes of section 19 a provider of services discriminates against a disabled person if–

(a) he fails to comply with a section 21 duty imposed on him in relation to the disabled person; and

(b) he cannot show that his failure to comply is justified.

Leaving aside the issue of justification, which will be dealt with later, the following example illustrates the operation of s.20(1):

> A party of adults has exclusively booked a restaurant for a special dinner. The restaurant staff spend most of the evening making fun of the party and provide it with worse service than normal. The fact that there are no other diners in the restaurant that evening does not mean that the disabled people have not been treated less favourably than other people. Other diners would not have been treated in this way.[140]

The concept of discrimination outlined here clearly requires proof that the disabled person has been treated less favourably than other persons without the disability, and requires a comparison of how the disabled person was treated relative to these other people. As Doyle notes:

> "The question is not merely whether the disabled person has experienced poor, inadequate or sub-standard provision in respect of goods, facilities or services. Rather the issue is whether there has been differential and unfavourable treatment of the disabled person in circumstances where other persons (to whom the reason related to disability does not apply) have not been so treated."[141]

---

140 *Para. 5.7, Code of Practice*

141 *Doyle, BJ, Disability Discrimination Law and Practice, Jordans, 5th ed. 2005, page 146*

The comparator is another member of the public, although the wording of the Act does not appear to rule out differential treatment by service providers among disabled people. Doyle provided the following example in a previous edition of his book:

> "If a group of variously disabled senior citizens sought to gain admission to a restaurant, but the restaurant refused to allow admission to the one member of the party using a wheelchair, while admitting his or her disabled colleagues, that could be unlawful discrimination, all other things being equal. It would be no defence to argue that the restaurant had admitted disabled persons. The individual would have been treated less favourably in comparison with other members of the public."[142]

There must be a causal connection between the discriminatory action and the complainant's disability. A disabled person who is refused admission to a hotel because he or she cannot to pay for the room, or who is refused service in the bar because he or she is drunk and disorderly, has not been discriminated against contrary to the Act. The reason for the less favourable treatment is not that person's disability, and, as Doyle points out[143], it is likely that the service provider would be able to show that any member of the public would also have been refused in similar circumstances and therefore there was no less favourable treatment at all.

There must be a connection between the less favourable treatment and a reason related to the disabled person's disability. Treating a disabled person less favourably for a reason related to his disability cannot be excused on the basis than another customer who behaved similarly (but for a reason not related to disability) would be treated in the same way. For example:

---

142 Doyle, BJ, *Disability Discrimination Law and Practice*, Jordans 1996, page 110

143 5th edition, p.146

"A group of deaf people who use British Sign Language (BSL) is refused entry to a disco. The doorman assumes that other customers might mistake communication using BSL as threatening gestures. This refusal of service is for a reason related to disability. It is likely to be unlawful even though the disco would have refused entry to anyone who made similar gestures."[144]

Nevertheless the Act cannot be used as a pretext for disruptive or anti-social behaviour unrelated to a person's disability. However spurious reasons cannot be used to refuse to serve a disabled person – even if the service provider thinks that serving the disabled person will upset or raise objections from other customers.

A service provider who makes the provision of goods, facilities or services subject to a requirement or condition, which a smaller proportion of disabled persons that non-disabled persons can meet, could be said to have *indirectly* discriminated against disabled persons if they suffer a detriment as a result and the service provider cannot justify the imposition of the requirement or condition in issue. The White Paper gives the specific example of a service provider banning animals from its premises and the disproportionate effect this would have on persons with visual impairments who rely upon guide dogs.[145] This would be a case that would clearly call for reasonable practical adjustments or modifications to be made by the service provider under s.21 of the Act.

Under s.20(2) a service provider discriminates against a disabled person if it fails to comply with a duty to make reasonable adjustments, unless the service provider can show that the failure to comply with the duty is justified. This is a separate form of discrimination from mere less favourable treatment. A service provider should not be able to justify discrimination without first demonstrating compliance or attempted compliance with a s.21 duty to make reasonable adjustments.

---

144 *2002 Code of Practice Para. 3.9,*

145 *See Glover v Hannah's Cafe (County Court Case No: MA202633) (www.drc-gb.org). Cf DRC013706 (www.drc-gb.org)*

The duty to make reasonable adjustments – s.21

What makes the DDA different from other law on discrimination is the requirement in it to take positive action to make reasonable adjustments for disabled persons. There are three aspects to this duty:

- the changing of practices, policies and procedures
- the provision of auxiliary aids
- the need to overcome physical features by
  - removing the feature
  - altering it
  - avoiding it
  - providing the service by an alternative method

The first two of these duties came into force early but the duty to make physical adjustments was not implemented until 2004.

As White notes[146], there are four key principles which underlie the duty to make adjustments. First, it is a duty to disabled people at large. Secondly, the duty has an anticipatory element, as it requires service providers to plan ahead to meet the needs of disabled people whether or not they already have disabled customers. Thirdly it is a continuous and evolving duty which needs to be reviewed in the light of changing circumstances, such as technological developments. Finally, although it is a duty at large, it is designed to give rights to individuals.

Regulations may make provision as to the circumstances in which it is reasonable for a service provider to have to take such steps. The duty will be subject to a costs limitation and the duty will not require the service provider to take any steps which would cause expenditure to be incurred exceeding a maximum sum yet to be prescribed by regulation (s.21(7)).

A failure to comply with the statutory duty to make reasonable adjustments is treated as amounting to discrimination against the

---

146 *White, J, DDA: Service Providers' Duty to make Reasonable Adjustments, Equal Opportunities Review No. 88, November/December 1999, page 33*

disabled person (s20(2)). These provisions were brought into force on 1 October 1999. The 1995 White Paper thought that it would not be enough simply to prohibit discriminatory behaviour. Legislation would also require:

> "positive action which is reasonable and readily achievable to overcome the physical and communication barriers that impede disabled people's access"[147]

(i) Practices, policies or procedures – section 21(1)

Section 21(1) provides:

> Where a provider of services has a practice, policy or procedure which makes it impossible or unreasonably difficult for disabled persons to make use of a service which he provides, or is prepared to provide, to other members of the public, it is his duty to take such steps as it is reasonable, in all the circumstances of the case, for him to have to take in order to change that practice, policy or procedure so that it no longer has that effect.

A service provider might have a practice which, perhaps unintentionally, makes it impossible or unreasonably difficult for disabled people to make use of its services. In such a case the service provider must take such steps to change the practice so that it no longer has that effect. This may simply mean instructing staff to waive a practice or amend a policy to allow exceptions or abandoning it altogether. The Code provides the following example:

> "A restaurant has a policy of refusing entry to male diners who do not wear a collar and tie. A disabled man who wishes to dine in the restaurant is unable to wear a tie because he has psoriasis (a severe skin complaint) of the face and neck. Unless the restaurant is prepared to waive its policy, its effect is to exclude the disabled customer from the restaurant. This is likely to be unlawful."[148]

---

147 *White Paper para 4.4*

148 *Para. 5.5, 2002 Code of Practice*

One likely example that will be caught by s.21(1) is the policy or practice of places which serve food and drink which exclude access to dogs accompanied by their owners. A number of these establishments already voluntarily make an exception for guide dogs accompanied by a visually impaired person. Similarly, a restaurant which refuses or limits access to wheelchair users will have to rethink this practice in the light of s.21(1).

In many cases, it is appropriate to ask customers to identify whether they have any particular requirements and, if so, what adjustments need to be made.

(ii) The duty to provide auxiliary aids – section 21(4)

Section 21(4) provides:

(4) Where an auxiliary aid or service (for example, the provision of information on audio tape or of a sign language interpreter) would –

(a) enable disabled persons to make use of a service which a provider of services provides, or is prepared to provide, to a member of the public, or

(b) facilitate the use by disabled persons of such a service,

it is the duty of the provider of that service to take such steps as it is reasonable, in all the circumstances of the case, for him to have to take in order to provide that auxiliary aid or service.

The term 'auxiliary aid or service' is illustrated in the Act by reference to the provision of information on audio tape or the provision of a sign language interpreter (s.21(4)). Further examples could include large print menus or audio-visual telephones in hotel rooms or websites adapted for the use of visually impaired visitors. However in many cases it may be sufficient to allocate a particular member of staff to provide requested assistance to a disabled guest. The 1995 White Paper envisaged that auxiliary aids will have to be provided where this is reasonable and readily achievable 'given the size, resources and the nature of the business' [149] These words do not appear in the Act itself, but the intention appears to be that what is reasonable must be judged taking account of all the circumstances of the case, and the interests of both parties are to be weighed in the balance. The Code provides the following example:

"A restaurant changes its menus daily. For that reason it considers it is not practicable to provide menus in alternative formats, such as Braille. However its staff spend a little time reading out the menu for blind customers and the restaurant ensures that there is a large print copy available. These are likely to be reasonable steps for the restaurant to have to take."[150]

(iii) Physical features – s.21(2)

Section 21(2) provides:

(2) Where a physical feature (for example, one arising from the design or construction of a building or the approach or access to premises) makes it impossible or unreasonably difficult for disabled persons to make use of such a service, it is the duty of the provider of that service to take such steps as it is reasonable, in all the circumstances of the case, for him to have to take in order to–

(a) remove the feature;

(b) alter it so that it no longer has that effect;

(c) provide a reasonable means of avoiding the feature; or

(d) provide a reasonable alternative method of making the service in question available to disabled persons.

---

149 *White Paper para 4.4*

150 *Para. 5.26, 2002 Code of Practice*

The definition of physical features is given a broad meaning by Regulation:[151]

9. For the purposes of sections 21(2) and 21E(3) of the 1995 Act, the following are to be treated as physical features (whether permanent or temporary)–

(a) any feature arising from the design or construction of a building on the premises occupied by the provider of services or by the public authority carrying out its functions;

(b) any feature on the premises occupied by the provider of services or by the public authority carrying out its functions of any approach to, exit from or access to such a building;

(c) any fixtures, fittings, furnishings, furniture, equipment or materials in or on the premises occupied by the provider of services or by the public authority carrying out its functions;

(d) any fixtures, fittings, furnishings, furniture, equipment or materials brought by or on behalf of the provider of services or by or on behalf of the public authority carrying out its functions on to premises (other than the premises that they occupy)–

(i) in the course of providing services to the public or to a section of the public or in the course of carrying out its functions,

(ii) for the purpose of providing such services or carrying out such functions;

(e) any other physical element or quality of any land comprised in the premises occupied by the provider of services or public authority carrying out its functions.

---

151 *The Disability Discrimination (Service Providers and Public Authorities Carrying Out Functions) Regulations 2005 SI No. 2901, 2005*

As the Code of Practice points out this would include:

> ... steps, stairways, kerbs, exterior surfaces and paving, parking areas, building entrances and exits (including emergency escape routes), internal and external doors, gates, toilet and washing facilities, public facilities (such as telephones, counters or service desks), lighting and ventilation, lifts and escalators, floor coverings, signs, furniture, and temporary or movable items (such as equipment and display racks).[152]

Under these provisions hotels will need to give consideration to a range of possible adjustments to physical features such as poorly designed or sited signage, restaurant seating, and the height and design of reception counters.

The following examples, adapted from the Code, are of clear relevance to hotels:

> [A club] has a high bar making it unreasonably difficult for wheelchair users to be served at the bar. The club lowers the bar so that wheelchair users can be served more easily. This is likely to be a reasonable step to have to take.[153]

> The changing facilities for women in a [hotel] gym are located in a room that is only accessible by stairs. The service provider suggests to disabled users of the gym with mobility impairments that they can change in a corner of the gym itself. This is unlikely to be a reasonable alternative method of making the service available, since it may significantly infringe upon their dignity.[154]

What is 'unreasonably difficult'?

The DDA does not define what is meant by 'unreasonably difficult'. The Code suggests that service providers should take account of

---

152 *Para. 7.45*
153 *Para. 7.48*
154 *Para. 7.51*

"whether the time, inconvenience, effort, discomfort, anxiety or loss of dignity entailed in using the service would be considered unreasonable by other people if they had to endure similar difficulties".[155]

An example could be customers who wish to check out at a busy hotel reception desk and have to queue to do so. A disabled customer with severe arthritis experiences great pain if he has to stand for more than a couple of minutes. Other customers would not expect to have to undergo similar discomfort in order to pay their bill.

Reasonableness

Adjustments are not required if they are not reasonable. Although the Government has power to cap service providers' expenditure on adjustments (s.21(7)) it does not propose to use it on the basis that the requirements of reasonableness is an adequate constraint. The decision as to what is a reasonable step for a particular service provider will depend on all the circumstances of the case including the type of services provided, the nature and size of the service provider and the effect of a particular disability.

The Code lists some of the factors which might be taken into account while stressing that the list is not exhaustive:[156]

● the effectiveness of any particular steps in overcoming the difficulty;
● the extent to which it is practicable for the service provider to take the steps;
● the financial and other costs of making the adjustments;
● the extent of any disruption caused by taking the steps;
● the extent of the service provider's financial and other resources;
● the amount of any resources already spent on making adjustments;
● the availability of financial or other assistance.

---

155 *Para. 6.35*
156 *Para. 6.25*

Fundamental nature of the services

A service provider is not required to do anything which would fundamentally alter the nature of its service or business (s.21(6)). Thus a night club with low-level lighting is not required to adjust the lighting to accommodate customers who are partially sighted if this would fundamentally change the atmosphere or ambience of the club.[157]

Effect of failure to make adjustments

A disabled person is able to make a claim against a service provider if:

● the service provider fails to do what is required; and

● that failure makes it impossible or unreasonable difficult for that disabled person to access any services provided; and

● the service provider cannot show that such a failure is justified.

The absence of any adjustment for the individual does not necessarily mean that the service provider has failed in its duty. It is conceivable that the particular requirements of the individual were not within the range of adjustments that the service provider could reasonably have made at the relevant time.

Justification

As indicated above, section 20 provides a defence of justification – both to less favourable treatment under s. 19 and for failure to comply with the duty to make reasonable adjustments under s.21. The justification however must fall within s.20(3):

(a) in the opinion of the provider of services, one or more of the conditions mentioned in subsection (4) are satisfied; and

(b) it is reasonable, in all the circumstances of the case, for him to hold that opinion.

The conditions in s.20(4) are that:

● The treatment is necessary on health and safety grounds (s.20(4)(a))

---

157 *White, page 36. Code of Practice Para. 10.39*

- The disabled person lacks the necessary capacity to enter into an agreement (s.20(4)(b))

- In refusing to provide the service (as under s.19(1)(a)) the treatment is necessary because otherwise it would not be possible to provide the service to other members of the public (s.20(4)(c))

- In discriminating in the standard of service or terms on which the service is offered (as under s.19(1)(c)&(d)) it is necessary to do so in order to be able to provide the service to the disabled person or to other members of the public (s.20(4)(d))

- In discriminating in the terms on which the service is offered (as under s.19(1)(d)) the difference reflects the greater cost of providing the service to disabled persons. (s.20(4)(e))

This justification defence, which is an integral part of the definition of discrimination, differs significantly from the parallel defence in the employment provisions in Part II of the Act. As the Government recognised:

> "service providers often have to take very quick and perhaps less informed decisions when serving someone [so that] an opinion-based approach remains appropriate" [158]

However, as can be seen, this 'opinion-based' approach comprises both subjective and objective elements. The discriminatory treatment of a disabled person will be justified only if, in the service provider's opinion, one or more statutory conditions are satisfied (s20(3)(a) (the subjective test) and it is reasonable in all the circumstances of the case for the service provider to hold that opinion (s20(3)(b) (the objective test). While an opinion-based approach was seen as appropriate:

> "the proper degree of objectivity is imposed because the opinion must be shown to be reasonably held"[159]

The Code of Practice states that a service provider does not have to be an expert on disability, but is expected to take account of all the

---

158 *HL Deb, vol 566, col 119 (Lord Henley)*
159 *HL Deb, vol 566, col 119 (Lord Henley)*

circumstances, including the information available to it, at the time. It will not be the reasonableness of the opinion itself that matters, but rather whether it was reasonable of the particular service provider to hold that opinion in the particular circumstances of the case.

Conditions for justification defence

The conditions which must be satisfied for the operation of the statutory defence of justification have been set out above. We will examine them in turn.

(i) Health or safety

Discrimination might be justified where the less favourable treatment is 'necessary' in order not to endanger the heath or safety of any person (s20(4)(a)). Thus a hotel leisure centre:

> "might be justified in excluding a disabled person from a beginners' swimming class if, by having to focus most attention on the disabled learner, the safety of other members of the class would be put at risk." [160]

It remains to be seen how this defence of justification will be interpreted and applied in practice. Health or safety risks have in the past been relied upon by service providers to exclude disabled persons from restaurants and theatres. Reference has often been made to the requirements of fire regulations.[161] The use of the word 'necessary' in s.20(4)(a) will call for individual justification on the facts where a service provider seeks to rely upon health and safety as the grounds for compromising the civil rights of disabled citizens.[162]

---

160 *HL Deb, vol 566, col 1025 (Lord Mackay of Ardbrecknish)*

161 *Restrictions produced by genuine requirements of local fire regulations will excuse otherwise discriminatory treatment by virtue of s 59 (actions done in pursuance of a statutory authority).*

162 *Doyle, BJ, Disability Discrimination Law and Practice, Jordans, 5th ed. 2005, page 163*

(ii) Incapacity to contract

The less favourable treatment of a disabled person can be justified if the disabled person is incapable of entering into an enforceable agreement, or of giving an informed consent (s.20(4)(b)). The Government's view at the time the bill was debated was that:

> "If a service provider has a reasonably held view that a contract with a disabled customer might be invalid, he must be allowed, under this measure, to refuse to enter into an agreement until it is reasonably clear that it would be enforceable, without the fear of being accused of discrimination." [163]

This would allow a hotelkeeper to refuse to enter into a contract with a disabled person, such as booking a wedding reception, if they hold a reasonably held opinion that the customer lacks or might lack legal capacity. The test is whether it is reasonable to discriminate within the particular circumstances of the case.

(iii) Providing the service

Where the discrimination is a straightforward refusal to provide services, such less favourable treatment might be justified if it is 'necessary' (not merely reasonably necessary) because the service provider would otherwise be unable to provide the goods, facilities or services in issue to members of the public.

The Government believed that it had introduced a strict test for the application of this defence as s.20(4)(c) applies only:

> " ... in circumstances in which, if a service provider were to serve a particular disabled person, he would not be able to continue to provide a service at all".[164]

The Minister for Disabled People thought this would only apply in extreme and rare circumstances. It would not be sufficient that the

---

163 *HC Deb Standing Committee E, col 349 (Mr W Hague)*
164 *HC Deb Standing committee E, col 354 (Mr W Hague)*

person at the bar had caused an inconvenient queue because he or she had a communication difficulty which caused delay in advising the bar staff of his or her requirements. The service provider might be irritated by this, but could not use this as a reason to justify refusing to continue serving that disabled person. Similarly a restaurant could not refuse to serve a party of customers with visible disabilities because other customers might object to their presence. The preferences of other customers are not a justification for discrimination.

(iv) Standard of service

This refers to the standard of service provided to disabled persons and the provision is similar to the third condition above and is likely to be applied in a similar fashion. Thus a restaurant which reserves certain seats for persons with mobility disabilities might rely upon this provision to justify what might amount to a differential standard or manner of service. The hotelkeeper might argue that it could not admit such a disabled person at all without infringing fire regulations or would otherwise cause great inconvenience to other customers. This example is given in the Code of Practice:

> "A hotel restricts a wheelchair user's choice of bedrooms to those with level access to the lifts. Those rooms tend to be noisier and have restricted views. The disabled person would otherwise be unable to use the hotel. The restriction is necessary in order to provide the service to the disabled guest. This is likely to be justified."[165]

(v) Greater expense

Discrimination on the terms on which services are provided may be capable of being justified where the difference in such terms 'reflects the greater cost to the service provider in providing the goods, facilities or services to the disabled person' (s.20(4)(e)). The Minister of Disabled People gave as an example a shoe-maker asked to make a shoe for a disabled person to an unusual design or in an unusual fabric. If the task would involve greater labour or special equipment or

---

165 *Para. 10.46*

material, it might be reasonable for the shoe-maker to charge the disabled customer a premium to reflect that.

A service provider should not provide a service to a disabled person on terms which are worse than the terms offered to other people, without justification. Worse terms include charging more for goods or imposing extra conditions. The Act does not prohibit positive action in favour of disabled people. Therefore service providers may provide service on more favourable terms to a disabled person.

However this last condition might be seen to justify an hotelkeeper charging a disabled person a room supplement for providing him or her with a room adapted to take a wheelchair or with an audio-visual fire alarm. The Government has clarified this point by stating that a service provider who attempts to pass on the costs of compliance with the Act to disabled persons (as opposed to spreading those costs across all customers) would not be facilitated in doing so by s.20(4)(e). The Code gives the example of a guest house which installs an audio-visual fire alarm in one of its rooms for visitors with a sensory impairment.[166] The guest house cannot legitimately charge more for this room (if it is otherwise identical to the other rooms) since it installed the fire alarm under its duty of adjustment. An assurance was given that the Act does not permit surcharges upon disabled persons for extra expenses or opportunity costs incurred by service providers in complying with the legislation.[167]

In addition, s.20(5) provides that any increase in the cost of providing a service to a disabled person which results from the service provider's compliance with a s.21 duty to make reasonable adjustments is to be disregarded for the purpose of s.20(4)(e). Service providers will not be able to directly pass on to disabled customers the costs of complying with the duties under the new legislation.

---

166 *Para 6.31*
167 *HC Deb Standing Committee E, col 357 (Mr W Hague).*

Guidance on adjustments

Once a service provider has decided to put a reasonable adjustment in place, it is important to draw its existence to the attention of disabled people. The service provider should also establish a means for letting the disabled person know how to request assistance. This might be done by a simple sign or notice at the entrance or at a service point, or in publicity materials. In all cases, it is important to use a means of communication which is itself accessible to disabled people.

Enforcement, remedies and procedures

A claim of unlawful discrimination in relation to Part III of the Act is the subject of civil proceedings for tort in the county court.[168] The usual remedy is compensation for financial loss but the court can also award damages for injury to feelings.[169] While most cases are likely to fall into the small claims jurisdiction, limited to £5,000, there is presently no limit for damages for injury to feelings. A plaintiff might also be entitled to seek a declaration confirming the parties' rights or an injunction (s.25(5)) requiring the service provider either to do something or stop repeating the discrimination.

Sex and Race Discrimination

Unlike the DDA the Sex Discrimination Act 1975 (SDA) and the Race Relations Act 1976 (RRA) do not impose positive duties on the hotelkeeper to modify his treatment of women and blacks in the same way as he must do for disabled persons. Also in common with the DDA there is very little in the way of case law in respect of racial and gender discrimination in relation to services in general and even less in relation to hotelkeeping in particular.

In keeping however with the philosophy of this book which is to provide source materials as well as an account of the law we shall quote extensively from the legislation and what little case law there is. Interestingly, although the sex and race legislation does not impose the

---

168 *DDA s.25(1)*
169 *DDA s.25(2)*

same requirement to take positive action as the DDA, nevertheless it nicely complements the common law duty by providing express statutory obligations. It probably goes further than the common law in some ways. The common law may require an hotelkeeper to take in all comers without discriminating but it does not necessarily prevent the hotelkeeper from discriminating between guests once they have arrived, by, for instance, offering inferior rooms, inferior standards of service and limited access to some parts of the hotel to women or blacks. Many hotels offer a range of services and facilities that go beyond basic bed and board, such as health clubs, swimming pools, bars, clubs and sports facilities, and it is in these marginal or peripheral activities that the legislation can be seen to be biting most significantly

The Sex Discrimination Act

The scheme of the Act is first to define what is meant by sex discrimination and then to go on to apply that definition to a variety of different activities – employment, education, provision of services and the disposal and management of property. Provision is also made for enforcement and for the establishment of the Equal Opportunities Commission, a body charged with promoting equal opportunities. We are concerned here primarily with the definition and how it applies to the provision of services.

The Definition

The meaning of sex discrimination can be found in s.1:

1. Direct and indirect discrimination against women

(1) In any circumstances relevant for the purposes of any provision of this Act ... a person discriminates against a woman if—

(a) on the ground of her sex he treats her less favourably than he treats or would treat a man, or

(b) he applies to her a requirement or condition which he applies or would apply equally to a man but—

(i) which is such that the proportion of women who can comply with it is considerably smaller than the proportion of men who can comply with it, and

(ii) which he cannot show to be justifiable irrespective of the sex of the person to whom it is applied, and

(iii) which is to her detriment because she cannot comply with it.

Section 1(a) contains the definition of direct discrimination – which would prevent an hotelkeeper refusing to accept a female guest simply because she was female. Section 1(b) covers indirect discrimination and covers more subtle forms of discrimination. A notice saying for example 'No persons with bare legs will be served in the hotel bar' might very well amount to sex discrimination in a city centre hotel where the proportion of women likely to be able to comply will be less than the proportion of men. However in a beachfront resort hotel it may not be discriminatory.

The Provision of Services

The definition of services expressly encompasses hotelkeeping within its scope:

s.29 Discrimination in provision of goods, facilities or services

(1) It is unlawful for any person concerned with the provision (for payment or not) of goods, facilities or services to the public or a section of the public to discriminate against a woman who seeks to obtain or use those goods, facilities or services—

(a) by refusing or deliberately omitting to provide her with any of them, or

(b) by refusing or deliberately omitting to provide her with goods, facilities or services of the like quality, in the like manner and on the like terms as are normal in his case in relation to male members of the public or (where she belongs to a section of the public) to male members of that section.

(2) The following are examples of the facilities and services mentioned in subsection (1)—

(a) access to and use of any place which members of the public or a section of the public are permitted to enter;

(b) accommodation in a hotel, boarding house or other similar establishment;

(c) facilities by way of banking or insurance or for grants, loans, credit or finance;

(d) facilities for education;

(e) facilities for entertainment, recreation or refreshment;

(f) facilities for transport or travel;

(g) the services of any profession or trade, or any local or other public authority.

(3) For the avoidance of doubt it is hereby declared that where a particular skill is commonly exercised in a different way for men and for women it does not contravene subsection (1) for a person who does not normally exercise it for women to insist on exercising it for a woman only in accordance with his normal practice or, if he reasonably considers it impracticable to do that in her case, to refuse or deliberately omit to exercise it.

Section of the public

Section 29 of the Act only applies where services are offered 'to the public or a section of the public'. The rationale for this is that the Act is not to be used to regulate the activities of 'genuinely private social clubs and other personal and private relationships.'[170] Given that hotels are, by definition, open to all comers this should not be an issue. Should an establishment that purports to be an hotel choose to discriminate against women on the grounds that it was not offering its services to the public then it would lose its status as an hotel – and the privileges and obligations that go with that status.

Caselaw

Gill v El Vino[171] is the leading case on sex discrimination in the provision of services. The facts of the case were that the plaintiffs, who were both women, entered the defendant's wine bar where they asked for two glasses of wine. In accordance with the defendant's rule that women were not allowed to stand and drink at the bar or in the bar area the barman refused to serve them at the bar and told them that if they sat at a table the drinks would be brought to them. There were two tables by the main entrance, and a smoking room at the back where a waitress took orders from customers at the tables. The chairs and table were also available to male customers. On an action by the plaintiffs alleging that the defendants' practice was in breach of the SDA it was held on appeal to the Court of Appeal that they had been discriminated against.

The character of the bar was described by Griffiths LJ:

"El Vino's is no ordinary wine bar, it has become a unique institution in Fleet Street. Every day it is thronged with journalists, solicitors, barristers exchanging the gossip of the day. No doubt it is the source of many false rumours which have dashed the hopes of many an aspirant to a High Court appointment. Now if a man wishes to take a

---

170 *Equality for Women, Cmnd 5724 (1974) para 66.*
171 *[1983] QB 425*

drink in El Vino's he can drink, if he wishes, by joining the throng which crowds round the bar and there he can join his friends and pick up, no doubt, many an interesting piece of gossip, particularly if he is a journalist. Or, if he wishes, he can go and sit down at one of the two tables that are on the right immediately behind the main door of the premises. Thirdly, if he wishes, he can pass through the partition and enter the little smoking room at the back, which is equipped with a number of tables and chairs. But there is no doubt that very many men choose to stand among the throng drinking at the bar.

But if a woman wishes to go to El Vino's, she is not allowed to join the throng before the bar. She must drink either at one of the two tables on the right of the entrance, or she must pass through the throng and drink in the smoking room at the back."

He then went on to hold that this amounted to discrimination:

"There is no doubt whatever that she is refused facilities that are accorded to men, and the only question that remains is: is she being treated less favourably than men? I think that permits of only one answer: of course she is. She is not being allowed to drink where she may want to drink, namely standing up among the many people gathered in front of the bar. There are many reasons why she may want to do so. Her friends may be there. She may not want to break them up and force them to move to some other part of the premises where she is permitted to drink. Or she may wish, if she is a journalist, to join a group in the hope of picking up the gossip of the day. If male journalists are permitted to do it, why shouldn't she? If she is denied it she is being treated less favourably than her male colleagues."

All three judges in the case regarded the issue as being relatively simple. Lord Eveleigh's comments are representative of the other two judges:

"It seems to me – and I do not apologise for going no further into the matter than saying "it seems to me" – that that is treating a woman less favourably than a man. It is as stark as that, and I find myself incapable of explaining further the reasons for that conclusion. I pose the question in the statute and in that way I answer it."

The Gill case was referred to in *McConomy v Croft Inns Ltd*,[172] an example of direct discrimination decided in Northern Ireland on legislation substantially similar to the legislation in England and Wales. The plaintiff, a man, had entered a bar which was part of an hotel wearing stud earrings and was asked by the manageress to remove them. When he refused he was escorted from the premises by two bouncers in a manner which he found embarrassing. He sued the proprietors on the basis that he had been treated less favourably than a woman. In the lower court it was decided that there was no discrimination – on the basis that the legislation did not require 'identical' treatment of men and women so long as the treatment was 'equal'. In particular, it was permissible, by reason of differing social conventions for men and women, to impose different standards of dress.

This line of argument was rejected on appeal. The judge had no doubt that there had been direct discrimination:

"It seems to me to be beyond question that the defendant's ground of refusal to serve the appellant in the bar while he was wearing earrings was that the appellant was a man. If he had been a woman it is common case that there would have been no objection to her being served while she was wearing earrings."

However that did not settle the matter because the court had to take into account Art. 7 of the legislation:

7. A comparison of the cases of persons of different sex ... under Article 3(1) ... must be such that the relevant

---

circumstances in the one case are the same, or not materially different, in the other.

In other words the court had to make sure that when making the comparison between the treatment of men and women under the legislation they were comparing like with like. On this the judge had to say:

" ... while I can see that in comparing like with like one would have to take account of certain basic rules of human conduct — such as the ordinary rules of decency accepted in this community — which might permit or require different dress regulations as between men and women, I find it difficult to see how in today's conditions it is possible to say that the circumstances are different as between men and women as regards the wearing of personal jewellery or other items of personal adornment."

A further argument that arose in the case was the issue of *de minimis* i.e. the case was so trivial that it should not have been brought at all. The judge clearly had some sympathy with this point of view:

"Since the possibilities of alleged discrimination in relation to the length and cut of hair, articles used for personal adornment, and dress generally, are endless in today's world I am very far from saying that the doctrine has no application in cases of alleged discrimination, and there must be some limit to the trivia with which courts and tribunals are asked to concern themselves."

However he felt constrained by the *El Vino* case where the Court of Appeal dismissed the 'de minimis' argument that was raised in that case in strong terms:

"We are enjoined to ask: was there a refusal of a facility? There clearly was. Can it be said that the refusal of that facility was a matter that could be classified as *de minimis*? In other words, it, seems to me that that involves saying 'well, she was less favourably treated but only very slightly'. I find it very difficult to evoke the maxim *de minimis non curat lex* in a situation where that which has been denied to the plaintiff is the very thing that Parliament seeks to provide." (Eveleigh LJ at p 431, *Gill v El Vino*)

James v Eastleigh Borough Council[173] is a case concerning differential entrance fees to a public swimming pool. It was the policy of the Council to offer free admission to their pools for those of 'pensionable age'. In practice, given the different ages at which men and women qualified for the state pension this meant that female bathers qualified for free admission at 60 but men had to wait until they were 65. The claimant sued on the basis that this contravened s.29 of the SDA. It was held by the House of Lords that this amounted to direct discrimination against men. It did not matter that the Council had not intended to discriminate against men, it was an objective test as to whether there was discrimination. The fact that the Council had chosen the state retirement age as the criterion for free entry did not help them as that was itself a gender-based criterion which directly discriminated between men and women, in that it treated women more favourably than men 'on the ground of sex' for the purposes of s.1(1)(a) of the 1975 Act. As indicated earlier, many hotels make their sports and health facilities available to the public. What this case does is to show that they should be careful in choosing the criteria on which they base entry and payment.

Guidance from the EOC

The Equal Opportunities Commission issues guidelines on what it considers to be discriminatory behaviour in relation to all aspects of the legislation.[174] Some of these guidelines are of relevance to the hotel industry, although it must be said that, as with the case law we have already examined, the discriminatory activities they describe relate more to the ancillary activities of hotelkeeping rather than the core activity of providing overnight accommodation.

---

173 *[1990] 2 AC 751*
174 *December, 2000.*

For instance, there are guidelines about admission to pubs and nightclubs which, as we have seen in the *McConomy* case, can impact upon hotel keepers. This is one of the examples they give:

"Is it lawful for a nightclub to admit women free of charge or give them free or reduced price drinks?

If a nightclub tries to attract women with free entry or free or reduced price drinks but charges men entrance fees and higher prices then this would be a breach of the SDA. In 1982 a man challenged a wine bar's practice of charging men £1 admittance fee but allowed women in free. A county court judge made a declaration that he had been discriminated against although only nominal damages were awarded."

Similarly it would be indirect discrimination for a club to offer free entry to 'anyone wearing a skirt' because fewer men than women could comply with the condition.

A further example provided by the EOC could be seen as applying to hotels that have car parks attached:

"My local town centre car park reserves prime spaces for women only. Is this lawful?

On the face of it, this practice is probably a breach of s.29 of the SDA as it is doubtful that an exception would apply in this instance. This is usually explained as being for safety reasons. However, this is unlikely to provide a defence under the SDA. Safety is in fact an issue for both sexes and large car parks should ensure that their premises are safe by installing CCTV cameras and improved lighting."

Race Discrimination

The Act

The scheme of the Race Relations Act is much the same as the SDA. It sets out what is meant by race discrimination and then applies the definition to a variety of activities including the provision of services.

The Definition

The meaning of race discrimination can be found in s.1:

S.1 Racial discrimination

(1) A person discriminates against another in any circumstances relevant for the purposes of any provision of this Act if—

(a) on racial grounds he treats that other less favourably than he treats or would treat other persons; or

(b) he applies to that other a requirement or condition which he applies or would apply equally to persons not of the same racial group as that other but–

(i) which is such that the proportion of persons of the same racial group as that other who can comply with it is considerably smaller than the proportion of persons not of that racial group who can comply with it; and

(ii) which he cannot show to be justifiable irrespective of the colour, race, nationality or ethnic or national origins of the person to whom it is applied; and

(iii) which is to the detriment of that other because he cannot comply with it.

(2) It is hereby declared that, for the purposes of this Act, segregating a person from other persons on racial grounds is treating him less favourably than they are treated.

As with the SDA, the Act defines both direct discrimination (in s.1(1)(a)) and indirect discrimination (in s.1(1)(b)). This issue was addressed in the case of *Commission for Racial Equality v Dutton*.[175] The facts of the case were that the defendant, the licensee of the Cat and Mutton pub in East London, displayed signs marked 'No travellers' at his public house. The reason for this was that previously he had been the licensee for a year at the Earl of Beaconsfield, in Southwark, and before that at the Lord Cecil, in Clapton. At both those houses he had had unpleasant experiences with people who came from caravans which were parked illegally on nearby sites. They had caused damage. They had threatened him and terrorised his wife. They had behaved generally in such a way as to upset his regular customers. So much so that, after such incidents, he had put up a sign in the windows of the Earl of Beaconsfield and, subsequently, the Lord Cecil, which read 'No travellers'. By that he had meant persons who travelled around in caravans and parked on illegal sites and gave him 'hassle'. He had wanted only to stop such people coming into his public house. Had the incidents continued he would have lost all his customers. After he put up the signs he had no more problems with such people. Following an incident involving persons from caravans parked near the Cat and Mutton he had put up a similar sign and had had no further trouble.

The Commission of Racial Equality, considering that the signs referred to gipsies so as to indicate an intention by the defendant to discriminate unlawfully against them, brought an action against him for a declaration that the signs contravened section 29(1) of the Race Relations Act – which makes it unlawful to publish an advertisement which indicates that a person an intention by a person to do an act of discrimination.

There were two issues in the case. The first was whether or not gipsies amounted to a racial group within the meaning of the RRA and the second was whether the notice amounted to direct or indirect discrimination against gipsies. The first question was answered in the affirmative. The second issue turned on whether the word 'traveller'

---

175 *[1989] QB 783*

was synonymous with 'gipsy'. If so, then there was direct discrimination under s.1(1)(a); if not, then it might amount to indirect discrimination under s.1(1)(b). The Court of Appeal came to the conclusion that this was possibly a case of indirect discrimination, but in the absence of any evidence on the point remitted the case to the County Court for a further hearing on the issue of whether the discrimination might be justified under s.1(1)(b)(ii).

Nicholls LJ gave these reasons for coming to the conclusion that there was no direct discrimination:

> "I can now state my reasons for agreeing with the judge's conclusion on the 'direct' discrimination issue. Like most English words, the meaning of the word 'traveller' depends on the context in which it is being used. It has one meaning when seen on a railway station. For some time now the refreshment service provided at railway stations and on trains has been styled 'Travellers Fare.' The word has a different meaning when in its context it is directed at travelling salesmen. In my view, in the windows of the Cat and Mutton 'No travellers' will be understood by those to whom it is directed, namely, potential customers, as meaning persons who are currently leading a nomadic way of life, living in tents or caravans or other vehicles. Thus the notices embrace gipsies who are living in that way. But the class of persons excluded from the Cat and Mutton is not confined to gipsies. The prohibited class includes all those of a nomadic way of life mentioned above. As the judge said, they all come under the umbrella expression 'travellers,' as this accurately describes their way of life.
>
> .....
>
> For this reason I cannot accept that the defendant's notices indicate, or might reasonably be understood as indicating, an intention by him to do an act of discrimination within section 1(1)(a). Excluded from the Cat and Mutton are all 'travellers,' whether or not they are gipsies.

All "travellers," all nomads, are treated equally, whatever their race. They are not being discriminated against on racial grounds."

On the question of indirect discrimination it had to be shown that all three conditions in s.1(1)(b) were satisfied, namely that proportion of gipsies who could comply with the condition, i.e. 'no travellers', was substantially smaller than the proportion of non-gipsies who could comply; that detriment was suffered as a consequence, and that the condition could not be justified. Nicholls LJ concluded that the first of these conditions was satisfied:

> "Clearly the proportion of gipsies who will satisfy the 'No travellers' condition is considerably smaller than the proportion of non-gipsies. Of the estimated gipsy population in the United Kingdom of some 80,000, between one-half and two-thirds now live in houses. But this still means that a far higher proportion of gipsies are leading a nomadic way of life than the rest of the population in general or, more narrowly, than the rest of the population who might wish to resort to the Cat and Mutton."

On the issue of detriment he was equally clear that it was satisfied. As for the third requirement, that the condition might be justified, the court had had no evidence on this and for that reason remitted it to the County Court for a re-hearing.

The Provision of Services

S.20 Discrimination in provision of goods, facilities or services

> (1) It is unlawful for any person concerned with the provision (for payment or not) of goods, facilities or services to the public or a section of the public to discriminate against a person who seeks to obtain or use those goods, facilities or services—
>
> (a) by refusing or deliberately omitting to provide him with any of them; or

(b) by refusing or deliberately omitting to provide him with goods, facilities or services of the like quality, in the like manner and on the like terms as are normal in the first-mentioned person's case in relation to other members of the public or (where the person so seeking belongs to a section of the public) to other members of that section.

(2) The following are examples of the facilities and services mentioned in subsection (1)—

(a) access to and use of any place which members of the public are permitted to enter;

(b) accommodation in a hotel, boarding house or other similar establishment;

(c) facilities by way of banking or insurance or for grants, loans, credit or finance;

(d) facilities for education;

(e) facilities for entertainment, recreation or refreshment;

(f) facilities for transport or travel;

(g) the services of any profession or trade, or any local or other public authority.

Again we can see that hotel accommodation is specifically referred to as one of the services where discrimination is prohibited.

Case Law

Another case involving gipsies which reached the House of Lords is the case of *Hallam v Cheltenham Borough Council.*[176] The facts of the case were that a Mrs Smith contracted with the Cheltenham Borough Council to hire the Pittville Pump Rooms in Cheltenham for a reception following the wedding of her daughter, the future Mrs Hallam, on 16 August 1997. The contract was signed well in advance, on the council's

---

176 *[2001] ICR 408; [2001] IRLR 312*

standard terms. Mrs Smith indicated that there would be about 150 guests. The husband of Mrs Smith and father of Mrs Hallam was of Romany gipsy origin, and so by descent was Mrs Hallam. The police in Gloucestershire had had some trouble with gipsies in the early months of 1997, and became concerned that there might be disorder at the reception which Mrs Smith was holding for her daughter. They communicated their concerns to the council. It was plain that the police had misunderstood some of the information which they had received, and the information which they gave the council was by no means accurate. But the council, sharing the fear of the police that the reception might attract large numbers of gipsies from all over the country, with a risk of disorder and serious damage to persons and property, sought to minimise the risk by unilaterally imposing new contract terms on Mrs Smith. One new term in particular Mrs Smith resented, a condition that entry to the reception should be restricted to those holding pre-issued tickets. She was unwilling to accept these terms and treated the council's conduct as repudiatory. The reception was held elsewhere.

The claimants sued the council for breach of contract and race discrimination, and the police for knowingly aiding the council to discriminate against them. It was the latter issue on which the case reached the House of Lords as the other two issues were decided by the County Court in favour of the claimants and were not appealed. That issue is not of immediate relevance to us. However this is how the discrimination issue was described in the House of Lords by Lord Bingham:

> "It is first necessary to ask: what is the act made unlawful by the 1976 Act which the council did? The answer is that the council denied to the appellants, because they were gipsies, the use of the Pump Rooms on the same terms as would have been available to others who were not gipsies and therefore treated the appellants less favourably than they would have treated others on racial grounds. Such conduct was made unlawful by sections 20 and 21 of the Act. So much is uncontroversial."

One other, early, case involving race discrimination and accommodation is *Webster v Johnson*,[177] a poorly reported case of apparently direct discrimination:

> Defendant landlady refused accommodation to the plaintiff, a Pakistani. As a result he was unable to join his white de facto wife and family in a holiday flat and had to take accommodation with his wife in a nearby hotel leaving the two children with the grandparents in the flat.

> Held, that (1) the refusal was the result of the defendant's consideration of her other customers' likely prejudices rather than her own views; (2) she did not know the plaintiff was the husband to the family; (3) the last two days of their holiday had been spoilt, although it was not the same as the case of a ruined holiday abroad in a bad hotel. The defendant had made a very handsome apology to the plaintiff in court. Award: alternative accommodation £15; additional meals £10; spoilt holiday £25; hurt feelings £25. Total award: £75.

It is difficult to draw any general conclusions from such a case but it is perhaps appropriate to conclude here with the comment that the case brings us full circle to *Constantine v Imperial Hotels Ltd*[178]where we began this discussion of discrimination. The reason given for discriminating against the plaintiff in *Webster v Johnson* was that the landlady was fearful of the prejudices of her other guests; in *Constantine* the reason for discriminating was that 'We will not have niggers in the hotel because of the Americans.' *Plus ça change.*

---

177 *[1979] C.L.Y. 740*
178 *[1944] 1KB 693*

CHAPTER FIVE
HOTELKEEPERS' LIABILITY FOR THE SAFETY OF GUESTS

A LEAP IN THE DARK

In previous chapters we have examined some of the fundamental concepts of hotel law – the definitions of what is an hotel and who is a guest, and the hotelier's duty to accept all comers. Now we turn to the hotelkeeper's obligations once the guest is over the threshold. What duties does an hotelier have in respect of the safety of his guests and for safeguarding their property, and what rights does he have over the guest's property in the event of not being paid.? In this chapter we look at the first of these duties – the hotelier's liability for the personal safety of his guests. The other issues are dealt with in later chapters.

Liability for the safety of guests can be conveniently divided into three aspects: liability in tort, liability in contract and product liability. The hotelier's liability in tort can again be subdivided into a number of other categories. If the guest is injured due to the state of the premises then liability will fall under the Occupiers' Liability Act 1957. If however the guest is injured by some activity carried on on the premises then any action will be based on simple common law negligence. This activity may be carried on by the hotelier himself or by his employees for whom he is vicariously liable.

In contract the liability will revolve around the supply of food and drink in which case the liability will lie under the Supply of Goods and Services Act 1982 which implies into every contract for the supply of goods a term that the goods, in this case food or drink, will be of satisfactory quality. This is not to say that there will not be an action in tort for the supply of substandard food but only that an action in contract is superior by virtue of the fact that the legislation imposes a strict liability standard rather than a standard of reasonable care.

Now that the European Directive on Product Liability[179] is part of English law, by virtue of the Consumer Protection Act 1987, hotelkeepers will also be under a strict liability for unsafe products supplied to their guests. This will, in the main, concern their liability for the food they serve to guests and will also overlap with their liability in tort and contract.

The Occupiers' Liability Act 1957

In very broad terms what the Occupiers' Liability Act 1957 (OLA) does is to impose a duty on 'occupiers', in this case hoteliers, to take reasonable care of 'visitors' (guests) who enter their premises. At first glance the statutory action under the Act appears little different, if at all, from an ordinary common law action in negligence. Often the boundaries between the two are so blurred that it really makes no difference whether the action is brought under the OLA or in negligence. For instance what if a waiter spills a drink and later a guest slips and falls as a result. Is the accident due to the defective state of the premises or the negligent failure to clean it up?[180]

The reason for this distinction is explained by North:[181]

"It might be asked, at the outset, why there were any special rules relating to occupiers' liability at all and why this whole area of liability could not be regarded as merely one aspect of the obligation of a person to take reasonable care not to cause injury to his neighbour founded upon Lord Atkin's famous dictum in *Donoghue v Stevenson* [1932] AC 562. The answer is historical. The basic pattern of the law relating to occupiers' liability was laid down in a number of important decisions at a time when general

---

179 *Directive 85/374/EEC*

180 *See Ward v Tesco Stores Ltd [1976] 1 WLR 810*

181 *'Occupiers' Liability', PM North, Butterworths, 1971, pp1–2*

broad principles of negligence liability were not fully developed. One may speculate that had negligence principles developed earlier, there might have been no separate rules as to occupiers' liability and this "pigeon-hole approach" might have been avoided; but the fact remains that the existence of such rules as a highly specialised sub-category of negligence liability was never doubted."

And, as Weir[182] has pointed out, the basis and extent of the duty under the OLA differs from common law negligence:

"The manufacturer is responsible at common law for the condition of the ginger beer and the occupier is responsible by statute for the state of the premises: both are under a duty to take reasonable care. This equation is delusive, however, since the duties differ in their basis and in their extent. The manufacturer is responsible because he does make the thing dangerous, whereas the occupier is responsible because he can make the thing safe; the manufacturer's duty arises from his action, the occupier's from his capacity to act (he must because he can). And the extent of the duties differs. Unlike the manufacturer, the occupier is not just under a duty not to cause harm to people; he must prevent harm to them; he must mend the premises and tend the visitor. For example, he must protect the visitor against other visitors. Those other visitors of course owe a duty to everyone present or probably present, but that duty is only the standard one of not hurting them; they are not responsible save in so far as they make the place dangerous; the occupier must make it reasonably safe for the visitor, and is consequently liable for a culpable omission to do so."

---

182 *'A Casebook on Tort', Tony Weir, Sweet & Maxwell, 2000, p. 38*

Occupiers

Liability is placed upon 'occupiers' but this term is not defined in the Act and therefore we have to look to the common law for the meaning of the term. The leading case on the issue is *Wheat v Lacon*[183] where it was held that the test for who was an occupier was a matter of control. In the words of Lord Denning:

> "... wherever a person has a sufficient degree of control over premises that he ought to realise that an failure on his part to use care may result in injury to a person coming lawfully there, then he is an "occupier" ..." (at pp. 593–4)

In hotels where both ownership and day to day occupation are in the same hands this poses no problems, the owner is the occupier for the purposes of the Act. However it is not unknown for the ownership and the occupation of an hotel to be split, or even where it is not, for the owner/occupier of the hotel to concede the occupation of parts of the hotel to others such as concessionaires – shops, beauty salons, health studios etc. In such cases who is the occupier? This was just the problem that arose in *Wheat v Lacon* itself. The facts of the case, as taken from the judgment of Lord Denning, are as follows:

> " ... the 'Golfer's Arms' at Great Yarmouth is owned by the respondents, the brewery company, E Lacon & Co Ltd. The ground floor was run as a public house by Mr Richardson as manager for the respondents. The first floor was used by Mr and Mrs Richardson as their private dwelling. In the summer Mrs Richardson took in guests for her private profit. Mr and Mrs Wheat and their family were summer guests of Mrs Richardson. About 9 pm one evening, when it was getting dark, Mr Wheat fell down the back staircase in the private portion and was killed. Winn J held that there were two causes: (i) the handrail was too short because it did not stretch to the foot of the stairs; (ii) someone had taken the bulb out of the light at the top of the stairs."

---

183 *[1966] AC 552*

Lord Denning also summarised the legal issue:

> "The case raises this point of law: did the respondents owe
> any duty to Mr Wheat to see that the handrail was safe to
> use or to see that the stairs were properly lighted? That
> depends on whether the respondents were 'an occupier' of
> the private portion of the 'Golfer's Arms', and Mr Wheat
> was their 'visitor' within the Occupiers' Liability Act, 1957:
> for, if so, the respondents owed him the 'common duty of
> care'."

The problem was that the accident occurred in the private part of the premises where Mr and Mrs Richardson lived and where they invited their guests, not in those parts of the premises to which the public were invited. Did this mean that the owners of the pub were not the occupiers of that part of the pub? Had they ceded occupation and control of the back stairs to the pub landlord and his wife? This turned upon the nature of the agreement between the owners of the pub and Mr Richardson, the manager.

Under that agreement Richardson was required, in return for a weekly salary, to live on the premises, to sell ales and spirits and to obey all lawful commands of his employers. Without differentiating between the ground floor and the first floor, the agreement expressly provided that the owners could enter the property at any time to inspect its physical condition and the state of the liquor being sold. Furthermore Richardson was not to part with possession of the premises without the permission of the owners. In return for his services he was allowed to live rent free on the premises. As a privilege Mrs Richardson was permitted to take in paying guests.

On the basis of these facts the House of Lords held that the owners retained sufficient control over the premises for them to be regarded as occupiers. Lord Dilhorne was of the opinion that the owners occupied the whole of the premises through their employee (who was not an occupier) but the other judges were of the opinion that there was dual occupation by the owners and Mr Richardson.

Of crucial importance in the case was the precise nature of the agreement between the owners and the manager. It was this agreement which effectively defined the relative responsibilities of the two defendants and which led to the Court holding that the owners, by virtue of the agreement, retained sufficient control to make them occupiers. A different form of agreement, ceding more control to the manager, could very well have led to different legal consequences.

Fisher v CHT[184] is another case involving multiple occupation which may have some bearing on the liability of hotelkeepers. The fact of the case were that Crockfords, the first defendants, ran a club containing a restaurant which was managed and run under licence by the second defendants, Tolaini Brothers. Tolainis paid no rent to Crockfords but under the agreement allowed senior executives of Crockfords to have some free meals in the restaurant. Tolainis decided to redecorate the restaurant and employed the third defendants, the Plaster Decoration Co. Ltd, to do the work, although the electrical work would be done by their own electrician. Crockfords were not involved in the work but had a maintenance man on the premises who was ready to give a hand if asked. While the plaintiff, who was employed by the plasterers, was putting up new plaster-work he came into contact with a live electric light wire which was exposed on the ceiling. He received a shock which caused him to fall and injure himself. The wire had become live when Tolainis electrician had, without warning, switched on all the electrical switches leading to the restaurant.

The issue, as in *Wheat v Lacon*, was who was the occupier of the premises on which the plaintiff was injured. There was no doubt that both Tolainis, as occupiers, and the Plaster Decoration Co, as employers, were liable to the plaintiff but what about Crockfords? Were they liable as occupiers? The Court of Appeal held that they were:

> " ... I feel no doubt that Crockfords were the occupiers of the restaurant. It is true that they had granted a licence to Tolainis; and that Tolainis were having this work done; and that Tolainis were themselves occupiers of the restaurant.

---

184 *[1966] 2 QB 475*

> But it is quite clear that more than one person can be in
> occupation: see *Willis v Association of Universities of the*
> *British Commonwealth.*[185] Although Tolainis had the use of
> the restaurant, Crockfords still had the right to go through
> it. Indeed, one of their men might on occasions have to go
> through in order to get to a room below. Crockfords
> controlled the entrance door to the whole premises. No one
> could get in and out except through that door. I think that
> Crockfords, as well as Tolainis, were occupiers and under a
> common duty of care under the Occupiers' Liability Act,
> 1957, to all the visitors coming onto the premises; and they
> include Fisher. The plasterers, as employers of Fisher, were
> under a duty to use reasonable care in carrying out their
> operations to see that Fisher was not exposed to any
> unnecessary risk." (Denning MR, at 481)

The message of these two cases is clear for hotelkeepers. Even if they
permit other, independent, businesses to operate within their walls
they may nevertheless retain responsibility for the safety of their guests
who are injured while visiting the 'premises' of the other business.
Take for instance an hotel which licenses shops to trade on the
premises. If the hotel retains responsibility for the fabric of the shop,
the maintenance and the cleaning of the shop premises it is easy to see
how a guest could find the hotelkeeper liable if they are injured when
the ceiling falls in or they slip on an inadequately cleaned floor.

However it is important to note from the cases that the degree of
control may vary between the joint occupiers and this will have an
impact upon their liability. For instance in *Wheat* Lord Denning said:

> "Two or more may be 'occupiers'. And whenever this
> happens, each is under a duty to use care towards person
> coming lawfully on to the premises, dependent on his
> degree of control." (at 594)

---

185 *[1965] 1 QB 140*

And Lord Morris said:

> "It may therefore, often be that the extent of the particular control which is exercised within the sphere of joint occupation will become a pointer as to the nature and extent of the duty which reasonably devolves on a particular occupier." (at 599)

Lord Pearce gave the following example:

> "The safety of premises may depend on the acts or omissions of more than one person, each of whom may have a different right to cause or continue the state of affairs which creates the danger and on each a duty of care may lie. But where separate persons are each under a duty of care the acts or omissions which would constitute a breach of that duty may vary very greatly. That which would be negligent in one may well be free from blame in the other. If the Richardsons had a dangerous hole in the carpet which they chose to put down in their sitting-room that would be negligent in them towards a visitor who was injured by it. But the respondents could fairly say that they took no interest in the Richardson's private furnishings and that no reasonable person in their position would have noticed or known of or taken any steps with regard to the dangerous defect. If the construction of the staircase was unsafe that would be negligence on the respondents' part. Whether the Richardsons would also be negligent in not warning their visitors or taking steps to reveal the danger would depend on whether a reasonable person in their position would have done so. Once the duty of care is imposed, the question whether a defendant failed in that duty becomes a question of fact in all the circumstances."

In truth we are trespassing here on the next aspect of the discussion: given that a particular defendant can be said to be the occupier what is the duty owed to the claimant?

The Duty of Care

Unlike the definition of 'occupier', which can only be found by having recourse to the common law, the standard of care required of an occupier is to be found in the Act itself. It is set out in s.2:

> 2(1) An occupier of premises owes the same duty, the "common duty of care", to all his visitors, except in so far as he is free to and does extend, restrict, modify or exclude his duty to any visitor or visitors by agreement or otherwise.
>
> (2) The common duty of care is a duty to take such care as in all the circumstances of the case is reasonable to see that the visitor will be reasonably safe in using the premises for the purposes for which he is invited or permitted by the occupier to be there.
>
> (3) The circumstances relevant for the present purpose include the degree of care, and of want of care, which would ordinarily be looked for in such a visitor, so that (for example) in proper cases–
>
> (a) an occupier must be prepared for children to be less careful than adults; and
>
> (b) an occupier may expect that a person, in the exercise of his calling, will appreciate and guard against any special risks ordinarily incident to it, so far as the occupier leaves him free to do so.
>
> (4) In determining whether the occupier of premises has discharged the common duty of care to a visitor, regard is to be had to all the circumstances, so that (for example)—
>
> (a) where damage is caused to a visitor by a danger of which he had been warned by the occupier, the warning is not to be treated without more as absolving the occupier from liability, unless in all the circumstances it

was enough to enable the visitor to be reasonably safe; and

(b) where damage is caused to a visitor by a danger due to the faulty execution of any work of construction, maintenance or repair by an independent contractor employed by the occupier, the occupier is not to be treated without more as answerable for the danger if in all the circumstances he had acted reasonably in entrusting the work to an independent contractor and had taken such steps (if any) as he reasonably ought in order to satisfy himself that the contractor was competent and that the work had been properly done.

A feature of section 2 is that it not only lays down what the duty is, 'the common duty of care', it goes on, in s.2(3), to provide examples of circumstances to be considered when deciding what amounts to the taking of reasonable care. These are that occupiers can expect that children to be less careful than adults and that a person in the exercise of his calling is expected to guard against the special risks of that calling. The latter example, in that it does not apply to guests or travellers, is beyond the scope of the article but we will examine the content of the common duty of care, and the duty to children, in turn. We will also examine s.2(4) which permits an occupier to show he has discharged his liability by giving adequate warnings or by showing that it was the fault of an independent contractor.

(a) The "common duty of care"

What amounts to reasonable care in the circumstances is a question of fact and it is on this issue that most reported cases on occupier's liability are decided. One case we have already examined, *Wheat v Lacon*, was ultimately decided on the basis that the occupier was not in breach of his duty:

> "The only question that now arises is whether Lacons failed to take such care as in all the circumstances it was reasonable for them to take to see that paying guests of the

Richardsons would be reasonably safe in using the premises. Though the staircase which Mr. Wheat used was the back staircase and not the main one I think that Lacons would and should have realised that a visitor might use the back staircase. Did they negligently provide a staircase which it would be unsafe to use? I cannot think that they did. In daylight the staircase was quite safe to use. In the period of 20 years before the day Mr. Wheat fell there had been no accident on the stairs. In darkness the means of illumination was provided. I cannot think that there was a failure to take reasonable care on the part of Lacons. I do not consider that they were negligent in failing to contemplate and to eliminate the possibility that someone unfamiliar with the stairs might use them in the dark or when a light was not available and might, on the assumption that the end of the handrail marked the reaching of the lowest stair, take a step onwards without feeling or testing whether such an assumption was correct." [Lord Morris of Borth-y-Gest at 599]

Simply because it is a question of fact does not necessarily mean that coming to a decision is straightforward. A Court of Appeal decision, involving a more famous hotel, illustrates vividly the problem the courts can have in deciding whether on the facts of the case the defendant has exercised reasonable care or not. In *Ward v The Ritz Hotel*[186] the claimant was drinking on the balcony of the Ritz Hotel when he fainted and fell over the balustrade of the balcony and was badly injured. The Court of Appeal, in a split decision, overturned the decision of the court below and held that the defendants were in breach of their common duty of care. Giving the opinion of the majority McCowan LJ said:

"I am driven to the conclusion that on the evidence placed before the judge, and in the light of his findings that the plaintiff fell because he fainted, and that he would

---

186 *20 May 1992, Court of Appeal (Civil Division), (Transcript:Association)*

probably not have fallen had the height of the balustrade been raised after the floor was tiled, he ought to have concluded that the defendant did not take such care as in all the circumstances was reasonable to see that the plaintiff was reasonably safe using the hotel for the purpose for which he was invited."

Lurking behind the simplicity of these words however is an abundance of evidence from ergonomists and architects which persuaded at least two other judges that the hotel was not in breach of its duty and which was sufficiently ambiguous to justify taking the case to successful appeal in the Court of Appeal.

Sawyer v H & G Simonds [187]is another hotel case but where the decision went against the claimant. The facts were simple. The claimant had been drinking in the bar of the Ship Hotel when his bar stool slipped on some liquor which had been spilled on the floor. As he fell he put out his hand to break his fall and cut it on a broken glass on the floor – from whence the liquor had come. He sued the occupiers of the hotel for breach of the OLA. Veale J held that there was no liability. After reciting s.2 of the Act he said:

> "This did not extend to the duty of *insuring* the safety of the visitor. Of course it was dangerous to allow broken glass to lie about anywhere where the public came and went. Of course broken glass should be cleared up as soon as possible. But one could not clear up broken glass unless one knew that broken glass was there to be cleared. [Emphasis added]
>
> The occupier was therefore under a duty to keep a reasonable look-out for this type of danger. The accident had occurred at a busy time in the lunch hour on a Saturday. It was the duty of the hall porter to come in every 20 minutes to clear empty glasses, and if he had seen broken glass on the floor he would have removed it.

---

187 *(1966) 197 Estates Gazette 877*

> "Reasonable care" involved consideration of the nature of the danger, the length of time that the danger was in existence, the steps necessary to remove the danger and the likelihood or otherwise of an injury being caused. The mere fact that this unfortunate accident happened did not connote negligence. There was an adequate system in the hotel for looking out for this kind of danger. The danger of falling from a stool in this way was remote. The barman had no knowledge that glass was on the floor."

There is nothing particularly remarkable about this case except that it does make the point that the duty is fault based and that the occupier is not under a strict liability. This is an issue which will be discussed later because there is case law to suggest that prior to the passage of the OLA an hotelkeeper might be under a higher duty.

A number of cases involve guests who are injured at night. In *Campbell v Shelbourne*[188] the claimant made his way from his room down a darkened corridor at 11.20pm looking for a lavatory. He came to a door which he opened, thinking it was the lavatory door, but it opened upon a steep flight of steps, down which he fell. It was held that the hotelkeeper had been negligent in not keeping the passageway reasonably lighted at a time when guests might be expected to be using it. In *Stone v Taffe*[189] the claimant was leaving a club at 1.00am and fell down stairs that were unlit. It was held that the defendants were liable even though the stairs were perfectly safe during daylight:

> " ... was there any breach of the statutory duty of common care? Common sense without expert evidence supports the judge's view that this staircase was dangerous when unlit, in the sense required by s 2(2) of the 1957 Act, namely that Mr Stone was not reasonably safe in using the stairs for the purpose of getting down to the ground floor and out of the premises. Common sense required the installation of a light at the top of the stairs. Would the brewers have taken

188 *[1939] 2 All ER 351*
189 *[1974] 3 All ER 1016*

such care as in all the circumstances of the case was reasonable to see that Mr Stone would be reasonably safe in descending these stairs if they had not provided any lighting at all for them? I should have though that the question answered itself: unlit these stairs were unsafe and so was anybody descending them." (Stephenson LJ)

A case the other way is *Walker v Midland Rly Co*[190] where the facts were that a guest left his bedroom in the middle of the night to go to the toilet. There were properly lighted and easily accessible toilets in the same corridor, but he went into a dark 'service room', the door of which was shut but not locked, and fell down the unguarded well of a lift at the end of the room, and was killed. The 'service room' was not lighted or used at night, and visitors had no business there at any time. The Earl of Selborne LC said, at pp 489–490:

"On opening the door it was apparent that the room was absolutely dark, and it must have been at once perceived that the drip of water came from the place where the sink was, which the deceased left behind him as he advanced into the room. He nevertheless, instead of continuing his search along the corridor for a water closet properly lighted (which he would have found within a very short distance if he had done so), went into this dark room. It contained one or more tables, on the same side as the sink, and some luggage was lying on the floor; but with those things he does not seem to have come in contact. He made his way through the darkness to the further end, and there met the danger which cost him his life. I think it impossible to hold that the general duty of an innkeeper to take proper care for the safety of his guests extends to every room in his house, at all hours of night or day, irrespective of the question whether any such guests may have a right, or some reasonable cause, to be there. The duty must, I think, be limited to those places into

---

190 (1886) 55 LT 489. See also *Knight v GTP Dev. Co* [1927] 1 DLR 498 *on similar facts.*

which guests may reasonably be supposed to be likely to go, in the belief, reasonably entertained, that they are entitled or invited to do so. Unless there was evidence fit for the consideration of a jury that any guest in the position of the deceased would, in the darkness of night, have reasonable ground for believing this service room to be a water-closet, and for acting as he did, there is nothing else in the case which (as it seems to me) could make the respondents' omission to provide against dangers within that service room wrongful towards the plaintiff's husband or generally towards their guests. In considering whether there was any evidence of neglect of duty by the respondents, it would not, in my opinion be right to leave out of sight the fact that they did not so conduct their hotel as to drive their guests to grope about in dark places, or to explore unknown rooms in order to find water-closets. These conveniences were provided on that corridor in positions easily accessible, and easily discoverable by any guests in the circumstances of the appellant's husband, who might endeavour, with reasonable care and patience, to observe or to find them; and they were kept properly lighted at night."

(b) Children

As we have seen, one of the circumstances to be taken into account by occupiers, is that children may be less careful than adults. The problem here is that premises which are perfectly safe for adults may harbour all kinds of dangers to children – and these dangers are magnified for very young children where almost any object can be hazardous – stairs, lifts, doors, lamps, windows etc etc. Does this mean, as one oft-quoted case puts it, that the occupier is "practically bound to see that the wandering child is as safe as in a nursery?"[191] The answer is no, an occupier does not have to make his premises 'baby proof'. The occupier is not under a strict liability, and as far as very young children are concerned the courts have adopted an approach which seems to

---

191 *Latham v Johnson [1913] 1 KB 398.*

have found general acceptance. It arises out of the case of *Phipps v Rochester Corporation*.[192] In that case two young children, the claimant, who was aged five, and his sister, aged seven, had wandered on to some open ground on which the occupier had dug a trench. The claimant had fallen into it and broken his leg.

> "[An occupier] who tacitly permits the public to use his land without discriminating between its members must assume that the public may include little children. But as a general rule he will have discharged his duty towards them if the dangers which they may encounter are only those which are obvious to a guardian or of which he has given a warning comprehensible by a guardian. To every general rule there are, of course, exceptions. [An occupier] cannot divest himself of the obligation of finding out something about the sort of people who are availing themselves of his permission and the sort of use they are making of it. He may have to take into account the social habits of the neighbourhood. No doubt there are places where little children go to play unaccompanied. If the [occupier] knows or ought to anticipate that, he may have to take steps accordingly. But the responsibility for the safety of little children must rest primarily upon the parents; it is their duty to see that such children are not allowed to wander about by themselves, or at the least to satisfy themselves that the places to which they do allow their children to go unaccompanied are safe for them to go to. It would not be socially desirable if parents were, as a matter of course, able to shift the burden of looking after their children from their own shoulders to those of persons who happen to have accessible bits of land. Different considerations may well apply to public parks or to recognised playing grounds where parents allow their children to go unaccompanied in the reasonable belief that they are safe." (Devlin J)

192 [1955] 1 QB 450

On this basis an hotelkeeper can expect that adult guests with very young children can be expected to take primary responsibility for the safety of the children – and be expected to protect them against obvious dangers and dangers of which the hotelkeeper has warned the adult. However where the dangers are hidden, or where the danger would be a danger to an adult as well as a child then the hotelkeeper cannot hide behind parental responsibility.

Many hotels have swimming pools, some are supervised, some are not. It would clearly be advisable for hotelkeepers to warn parents that if the pool is unsupervised then children under a certain age will not be permitted to use the pool without an older person being with them. If, following such a warning, a young child suffered injury while unsupervised then the hotel would have a good defence where the injury was caused by an obvious danger – such as drowning. It might be different if, for instance the chemicals added to the water had been added in the wrong quantities and the child was poisoned.

Some hotels make themselves attractive to a family clientele – offering children's activities, child discounts, children's meals etc. Does this mean that an hotelkeeper cannot rely on parental responsibility in such circumstances. There is the merest hint of this in *Phipps* where Devlin J states that where an occupier can expect unaccompanied children to be wandering around his premises then he 'may have to take steps accordingly'. But this is heavily qualified and it is unlikely to mean that the hotel is liable if a guest allows his two year old child to wander out of sight and fall down the stairs. (See *Simkiss v Rhondda* (1983) 81 LGR 460 for an example of how the occupier escaped liability when a parent permitted a child to play on premises with an obvious danger.)

This approach is applied to 'little children'. If the child is older and therefore of an age to go about the hotel unaccompanied then it appears the hotelkeeper cannot fall back on parental responsibility. This suggests that there is an intermediate category of danger that the hotelkeeper should protect the older child against but not necessarily an adult. The danger would have to be relatively obvious to an adult but not to a younger child. For instance some hotel rooms contain kettles for guests to make their own tea and coffee. If a family booked a younger child into one of these rooms and an accident occurred with the kettle this might amount to negligence by the hotelkeeper – permitting a child to stay alone in a room with a kettle. The problem with this scenario is that, unlike with the little children who have been allowed to wander off without a parent, here the parent is present and presumably in *loco parentis*. In which case why should the hotel have a greater responsibility than the parent? Shouldn't the parent have removed the kettle or warned the child? The answer here is perhaps that with little children the hotelkeeper is not negligent because he could not expect such a young child to be unaccompanied by a responsible adult whereas in this case there is a *prima facie* case of negligence – the older child might be expected to go unaccompanied into the room without his parents and therefore be exposed to a danger which is not obvious to him. There may be an issue of joint causation and the hotelkeeper will not necessarily be relieved of liability.

Where the hotelkeeper has accepted the child as a guest at the hotel without the presence of a parent then the answer would almost certainly be that the hotelkeeper was liable.

(c) Warnings

The hotelkeeper can discharge his duty by providing warnings which are enough to enable the visitor to be reasonably safe (s.2(4)(a)). One of the leading cases on this issue is *White v Blackmore*[193] in which the claimant, who was attending a jalopy race, was killed when a car came through the safety ropes which had been erected in a negligent fashion by the organisers. Notices were displayed on the course which said "Warning To The Public. Motor Racing Is Dangerous". Lord Denning said of the notices:

> "The warning notices in this case do not enable the visitor to be reasonably safe. They do not tell him anything about any danger except that "motor racing is dangerous." They

---

193 *[1972] 2 QB 651*

do not tell him to avoid the danger by going away – for that is the very last thing the organisers want him to do. They want him to come and stay and see the races. By inviting him to come, they are under a duty of care to him: which they cannot avoid by telling him that it is dangerous."

If the notices had been more specific e.g. 'These rope barriers are insufficient to protect you from the cars. Please stand back 50 yards' that might have been enough to have enabled the claimant to have been reasonably safe.

Swimming pools, ponds and lakes are clearly a source of danger and there are a surprisingly large number of cases involving drownings where the occupier has faced action. A recent case is *Darby v National Trust*[194] where the claimant was drowned in a large pond on the defendant's property. One of the issues was whether or not the occupiers should have put up warning notices. May LJ said:

"In my judgment the risks to competent swimmers of swimming in this pond from which Mr Darby so unfortunately succumbed were perfectly obvious. There was no relevantly causative special risk of which the National Trust would or should have been aware which was not obvious. One or more notices saying 'Danger No Swimming' would have told Mr Darby no more than he already knew."

In other words putting up a warning sign warning of an obvious danger makes no difference. It merely tells the visitor what he already knows, and if the occupier is not to be regarded as negligent by permitting the swimming in the first place, a failure to put up a notice will not make him so.

Older hotels which do not comply with modern building standards where there are hazards such as steep winding stairs, uneven floors, low beams, unexpected steps etc may find that the only way to

---

194 *[2001] PIQR 27*

discharge their duty to take care is by providing adequate warning. Exposing guests to such risks and expecting them to fend for themselves would be negligent. A general warning to take care may not be sufficient; it may require someone to point out the hazards on an individual basis while guests are being shown to their rooms.

(d) Independent contractors

In English law it is the rule that employers are not liable for the tortious actions of their independent contractors. This rule has been incorporated into s.2(4)(b) of the OLA quoted above. Essentially what it says is that so long as the occupier has taken reasonable care in choosing an independent contractor and ensuring that the work has been properly done then he will not be liable to visitors so long as there is no independent negligence on his part.

The leading case on this issue and one which has clear implications for hotelkeepers is *Haseldine v Daw*[195] in which a lift in a block of flats failed and the claimant was injured. There had been negligence by the employees of the firm of engineers that had been employed to maintain the lift but the defendant landlord, the employer of the engineers, was found not liable. This is what Scott LJ had to say:

> "The invitor is bound to take that kind of care which a reasonably prudent man in his place would take – neither more nor less. The landlord of a block of flats, as occupier of the lifts, does not profess as such to be either an electrical or, as in this case, a hydraulic engineer. Having no technical skill he cannot rely on his own judgment, and the duty of care towards his invitees requires him to obtain and follow good technical advice. If he did not do so, he would, indeed, be guilty of negligence. To hold him responsible for the misdeeds of his independent contractor would be to make him insure the safety of his lift. That duty can only arise out of contract, as in the case of an employer's duty towards his employed which in certain

---

195 *[1941] 2 KB 343*

cases may make him responsible for the structural fitness of the premises where they are to work."

In the present case the landlord was ignorant of the mechanics of his hydraulic lifts and it was his duty to choose a good expert, to trust him, and then to be guided by his advice. I think that he realised his duty and wholly discharged it, so far as the safety of others was concerned, for he chose a first-class firm of lift engineers and trusted them, and over a long period of years and in connection with many lifts he found them trustworthy.

Cook v Broderip[196] is another case where the occupier escaped liability. The occupier of a flat had employed an apparently competent electrician to fit a new switch fuse. The work had been done negligently and the occupier's cleaner had been electrocuted as a consequence. It was held by the High Court that the occupier was not liable on the grounds that he had taken reasonable care in the circumstances:

"Major Broderip had taken reasonable care that persons coming to his flat would be safe from injury from electricity. If he had attempted to do the work himself and made a mistake, he would have had no answer to an allegation that it was negligent to attempt to do it himself and that he ought to have employed a competent contractor. He (the judge) could not think it good law that the occupier of a house or flat could not install an electrical circuit, or for that matter a central heating system, without underwriting the work of specialist contractors which he had no possible means of checking, should it be negligently done and cause injury to a domestic servant."

Liability might have been different in these cases if the independent contractors had turned out to be 'cowboys' who were obviously incompetent. For instance a hotel might employ contractors to

---

196 *(1968) 112 Sol Jo 193; 206 EG 128; [1968] EGD 210*

partially refurbish some of the rooms. If they are working in a corridor of rooms where guests are passing to and fro and they persistently leave rubbish and equipment in the corridor where unwary guests might trip over it and be injured then it would be difficult for the hotelkeeper to escape liability.

The extent to which the occupier must supervise the work of the independent contractor was raised in the case of *AMF International Ltd v Magnet Bowling Ltd.*[197] In that case the claimant had been installing bowling equipment in the occupier's property which was in the course of construction by an independent contractor. Due to the negligence of the independent contractor the property was flooded and extensive damage was done to the bowling equipment. Finding the defendants liable Mocatta J said:

> " ... s.2(4)(b) of the Act of 1957 contemplates that it may be reasonable to delegate work of construction or maintenance to an independent contractor. It is accepted, clearly rightly, that it was reasonable for Magnet to employ Trenthams [the independent contractors]. But the subsection also contemplates that in such circumstances, in determining whether the occupier has discharged the common duty of care, the court may further have to consider whether the occupier ought to have taken any steps to satisfy himself that the work had been properly done by the independent contractor. In the case of the construction of a substantial building, or of a ship, I should have thought that the building owner, if he is to escape subsequent tortious liability for faulty construction, should not only take care to contract with a competent contractor or shipbuilder, but also to cause that work to be supervised by a properly qualified professional man such as an architect or surveyor, or a naval architect or Lloyd's surveyor. Such cases are different in fact and in everyday practice from having a flat re-wired (as in *Green v Fibreglass Ltd* [1958] 2 QB 245).

---

197 *[1968] 1 WLR 1028*

Whilst these examples refer to completed work, I cannot think that different principles can apply to precautions during the course of construction, if the building owner is going to invite a third party to bring valuable property on to the site during construction. Whilst it may well be that an architect employed by a building owner to supervise construction by a builder has no power under the building contract to dictate how the builder is to perform the contract or what temporary steps he should take during construction to guard against flooding, nevertheless advice from the architect to the builder may have the desired effect. Above all, however, if the architect is dissatisfied with such precautions and cannot persuade the builder to improve them, he will be able to inform the building owner of the position. The latter will then be able not to invite the third party on to the site, or postpone the invitation, or, possibly, obtain the third party's consent to entry at his own risk. I think, therefore, Magnet should have taken steps, before inviting and allowing AMF to enter, to satisfy themselves that Trenthams had done their work properly including temporary anti-flood precautions, and there is no doubt they could have done this either by Mr. Bate or Mr. Smith [architects employed by Magnet]."

Essentially what he is saying is that the more complex, technical or dangerous the work the more care the occupier must take and in such cases it is not good enough simply to have employed a competent independent contractor, steps must also be taken to see that the work has been done properly. For a simple job such as a new electrical fuse Major Broderip was entitled to rely upon the competence of the contractor but for major refurbishments an hotel should be employing specialist professionals to supervise the work.

Defences

The two defences one would expect, contributory negligence and *volenti non fit injuria*, are both available to a defendant.

(i) Contributory Negligence

Interestingly, contributory negligence is not expressly provided for in the Act, but the courts have nonetheless been willing to apply it where appropriate.[198] The source of the defence is the Law Reform (Contributory Negligence) Act 1945 which provides in section 1(1):

> (1) Where any person suffers damage as the result partly of his own fault and partly of the fault of any other person or persons, a claim in respect of that damage shall not be defeated by reason of the fault of the person suffering the damage, but the damages recoverable in respect thereof shall be reduced to such extent as the court thinks just and equitable having regard to the claimant's share in the responsibility for the damage.

Stone v Taffe,[199] referred to earlier, also involved a finding of 50% contributory negligence on the part of the deceased. Unfortunately the precise grounds for this are not reported but reading between the lines it is presumably because the court felt that the claimant was not taking reasonable care of himself by descending unlit stairs in the dark after having been drinking.

In the Canadian case, *Clow v Tracey*,[200] there was also a finding of 50% contributory negligence by the claimant. The facts of the case were that while visiting the defendant's hotel for lunch the plaintiff went to the bathroom. There was a single step up into this room from the hall, and the wash-room was bright and sunny, in contrast to the hall. When the plaintiff left the wash-room she did not see the step down into the hall and fell, sustaining serious injuries. It was held that the defendants

---

198 *Slater v Clay Cross Ltd* [1956] 2 QB 264
199 [1974] 3 All ER 1016
200 [1949] O.W.N. 384; aff'd [1949] 4 D.L.R. 807

were guilty of negligence for not warning of the step. On the question of contributory negligence the judge had this to say:

> "Was the plaintiff guilty of contributory negligence? After a great deal of thought on the matter, I am of the opinion that she was. The plaintiff wears glasses, but I find that with them on, as they were on the occasion in question, her eyesight is excellent. She must have been aware, in entering the wash-room, that she had gone up a step. As will be seen from ex. 3, the door of the wash-room opens inwards. Although it was possible to stand between the wash basin and the edge of the door and open it, such a position would be quite unnatural and quite unlikely, and it is probable that the plaintiff opened the door fully before going out, and therefore found herself at least one or two paces from the edge of the doorway. She therefore should have observed that there was a step, even if she had forgotten about it. I do not think that the corridor was so dark that she could not observe the step. She just did not look.
>
> In modern hotels one might expect the floor of these rooms to be on the level of the corridors, but in these very old hotels such steps were the rule and they should be looked for by the travelling public."

(ii) Volenti non fit injuria

Volenti is provided for in s.2(5):

> (5) The common duty of care does not impose on an occupier any obligation to a visitor in respect of risks willingly accepted as his by the visitor (the question whether a risk was so accepted to be decided on the same principles as in other cases in which one person owes a duty of care to another).

It is generally accepted[201] that this is simply the common law defence

---

201 *E.g. Jones, Textbook on Tort, 8th ed., p.308; North, p.116.*

of volenti in statutory form and therefore imports all the common law concepts into the statutory scheme. One of the leading cases in occupiers liability on the issue of volenti is *White v Blackmore*,[202] the case involving the negligently constructed safety barriers at the jalopy race, referred to above. One of the defences was that the claimant had been volenti to the risk. Denning LJ had this to say on the application of the defence:

> "No doubt the visitor takes on himself the risks inherent in motor racing, but he does not take on himself the risk of injury due to the defaults of the organisers. People go to race meetings to enjoy the sport. They like to see the competitors taking risks, but they do not like to take risks on themselves. Even though it is a dangerous sport, they expect, and rightly expect, the organisers to erect proper barriers, to provide proper enclosures, and to do all that is reasonable to ensure their safety. If the organisers do everything that is reasonable, they are not liable if a racing car leaps the barriers and crashes into the crowd: see *Hall v Brooklands Auto Racing Club* [1933] 1 KB 205. But, if the organisers fail to take reasonable precautions, they cannot excuse themselves from liability by invoking the doctrine of *volenti non fit injuria*; for the simple reason that the person injured or killed does not willingly accept the risks arising from their want of reasonable care ...
>
> In this case Mr. White was quite unaware that the organisers had been negligent. He never willingly accepted the risk of injury due to this default. They cannot rely on *volenti non fit injuria*."

The case illustrates the principle that a claimant cannot be held to be volenti if he does not know of the risk. But even when the guest has knowledge of the risk it does not mean that they willingly consent to it. Take the example given earlier of the hotel refurbishment where

---

202 *[1972] 2 QB 651*

equipment and rubble is left in the hotel corridors. A guest passing along the corridor may know of the risk but they do not consent to it. They only expose themselves to the risk because that is the only way to their room. It might be different if for instance the hotel warned guests of the risk, cordoned off that part of the hotel and told guests to use an alternative route to their room. If a guest, in order to take a short cut to his room, decided to risk the cordoned off route and was injured while negotiating the rubble then a good case could be make out for volenti.

A Higher Duty?

The Occupiers' Liability Act imposes a duty to take reasonable care, not a duty to see that care is taken. In most cases this will not make a difference but when it comes to injuries caused to guests by independent contractors we can see how an occupier may escape liability, as in *Haseldine v Daw*, where the contractor is negligent but the occupier is not. In Ireland where the liability of hotelkeepers is governed by the Hotel Proprietors Act 1963 the situation may be different. The Act provides that hotelkeepers must ensure that, for the purpose of personal use by the guest, the premises are as safe as reasonable care and skill can make them.

McDonald[203] contrasts the position of hotelkeepers, who are governed by this higher duty, with publicans, who are not:

> "To illustrate the difference, let's imagine identical accidents to two non-residents, one in a public house toilet and the other in a hotel bar toilet. On pressing the button on the hand dryer, the customer's hands are burned by the air being excessively hot or perhaps by the machine falling off the wall and injuring the customer's foot. Let's also pretend the machine had been installed and serviced by a hand-dryer company and there was nothing visibly wrong with it which either the establishment or the customer could have been expected to notice. Let's further imagine that both

---

203 *Reform of the Hotel Proprietors Act 1963 [1999] ITLJ 156*

establishments had checked the competence or the hand-dryer company and that neither customer pressed the button so hard as to have possibly contributed to the accident.

In the case of the hotel, the effect of Section 4 of the 1963 Act is likely to be that the hotel will be liable to the customer for the carelessness of the outside contractor in installing/servicing the machine. The fact that the hotel could not have discovered the defect will be of no relevance to its liability to the customer, though the hotel will probably be able to pass some/all of its liability onto the hand dryer company.

By contrast, the possible effect of Section 7 of the 1995 Act on the public house is likely to be that it will not be liable for the customer's injury. Assuming care was taken in selecting the contractor and there was nothing evidently wrong with the machine and the public house had no reason to suspect anything, then it will not be liable.

Thus for two identical accidents the current laws carry the possibility of producing different results."

Prior to 1957 there were decisions at common law to the effect that in England and Wales the law was the same as it currently is in Ireland i.e. a higher duty than simply to exercise reasonable care in respect of guests' safety. In *Maclenan v Segar*[204] a guest was injured in an hotel fire when she tried to escape from her room using a makeshift rope of sheets and blankets. While descending she fainted and fell through a glass roof below. The cause of the fire was due to the negligently designed scheme for smoke and burning soot from the kitchens. The scheme had been designed and built by independent contractors – an architect and a builder. McCardie J held that the duty of the innkeeper was not simply to exercise reasonable care. The duty was higher than that: a warranty that the inn premises were as safe as reasonable care

---

204 *[1917] 2 KB 325. See also the Canadian cases Beaudry v Fort Cumberland Hotel Ltd (1971) 24 DLR (3d) 1 and Beauchamp v Ayotte (1971) 19 DLR (3d) 258 to the same effect.*

and skill on the part of any one can make them. Referring to previous cases he said that the rule in those cases was that:

> " ... it matters not whether the lack of care or skill be that of the defendant or his servants, or that of an independent contractor or his servants, or whether the negligence takes place before or after the occupation by the defendant of the premises."

Then he went on to say that:

> "In my opinion this rule applies to the present case."

The question is whether or not this case has survived the OLA, and if it has survived the Act then what is the rationale? To take the second question first, perhaps the only basis could be that the law of inns and innkeepers is clearly distinct from the ordinary law of contract and tort with its own distinct rules. We have seen this already in our discussion of the duties of an hotelkeeper to receive all comers – a duty which is imposed by the custom of the realm rather than conventional rules of contract. If it could be argued that 'guests' are not simply 'visitors' and that hotelkeepers are not simply 'occupiers' and that traditionally guests have been owed a higher duty than visitors, and that the OLA does not abolish this distinction then a case might be made out. Unfortunately the evidence is all against this. First, there is no support for this view in the judgment of McCardie J. He approaches the case from a conventional occupiers' liability perspective. The reason for imposing the higher duty was *not* that the claimant was a *guest* but because she entered the hotel as a *contractual visitor* and as such was owed a higher duty than a non-contractual invitee or licensee. There is nothing in this case, or any other case for that matter, to suggest that liability for the safety of guests is other than a simple tortious liability.

Secondly, and more tellingly, when the law of occupiers' liability was reformed in 1957 it was done on the basis of a Law Reform Committee report.[205] The report expressly considers the case of *Maclenan v Segar*.

---

205 *Law Reform Committee, Third Report, 'Occupiers' Liability to Invitees, Licensees and Trespassers', Cmd. 9305*

After a long discussion on the merits of imposing a higher duty in favour of contractual entrants, and if so, in what circumstances, the imposition of a higher duty (except where expressly provided for) was rejected in favour of a uniform standard simply to take reasonable care.[206] Again, there is nothing in the discussion which suggests that guests are owed a higher duty as such. When the OLA was enacted these recommendations were accepted by the legislature.

Thus it seems that despite *Maclenan v Segar* a guest is simply owed the 'common duty of care' under the Act and cannot take advantage of a higher duty.

Vicarious Liability

As well as primary liability under the OLA and in negligence the hotelkeeper may incur vicarious liability for the torts committed by his employees – predominantly negligence but occasionally trespass to the person i.e. assault and battery.

For the hotelkeeper to be vicariously liable the claimant has to establish that

- A tort has been committed
- By an employee
- In the course of his/her employment.

If we assume that it can be established that the employee has committed a tort, either negligence or trespass, then it is only the two remaining requirements that we need to examine.

Employees

The law distinguishes between employees and independent contractors. An employer, in our case an hotelkeeper, is liable for the torts of the former but not for the latter, therefore the distinction is crucial. The distinction is often referred to as the difference between a contract of service and a contract for services. In most cases this is a distinction which is easily made but at the margins there are acute difficulties.

---

206 *Paras 47–56*

The distinction is straightforward in the following examples. What if, for instance, the hotel employs a full time chambermaid, who negligently leaves soapy water in the shower tray and the guest slips and is injured. There is no doubt in these circumstances that the hotelkeeper will be liable for a negligent act committed by its *employee*. However if the hotel subcontracts its cleaning to a firm of independent cleaning contractors and one of the subcontractor's employees does the same thing there will be no liability. If the hotel employed a full time electrician who negligently left a live wire exposed in a bedroom and a guest was electrocuted the hotelkeeper would be liable, but would not be liable if a firm of electrical contractors had been employed to refurbish a room and one of their employees had done the same thing.

Note that if the hotelkeeper had had reason to believe that the employees of the independent electrical contractor were incompetent there would be liability on the part of the hotelkeeper – but this would not be vicarious liability this would be for the hotelkeeper's own negligence in failing to take care of its guests.

Difficulties may arise however if, for instance, the arrangement with the subcontractor is that it supplies the cleaners who are then dressed in the uniform of the hotel and who take instructions from the hotel's housekeeper and who work alongside other of the hotel's employees and who eat in the hotel's kitchen with other full time employees. In such a case the two employees are virtually indistinguishable for practical purposes and in such a complex situation the law too has trouble distinguishing between them for the purposes of liability. To cope with such situations the law has developed a number of tests over the years.

(i) The control test

Early cases stressed the extent of the control that an employer has over his employees. This is reflected in the case of *Collins v Hertfordshire CC*[207] where Hilbery J said:

---

207 *[1947] KB 598*

> "The distinction between a contract for services and a contract of service can be summarised in this way: In the one case the master can order or require what is to be done, while in the other case he can not only order or require what is to be done, but how it shall be done."

Conversely an employer was not in a position to tell an independent contractor *how* to do his job.

But what might be applicable to pre-industrial or early industrial economies is not necessarily appropriate to modern technological advanced societies where employees often possess skills and expertise such that their employers could not possibly control *how* they did their jobs. Employers could give broad directions on what is to be done but would be unable, and in many cases unwilling, to instruct the employee precisely how the work should be done. Examples that come readily to mind are surgeons, airline pilots and computer technicians. As a consequence the control test, while still retaining some significance, has been supplemented by other tests.

If we pause for a moment before looking at these other tests we will see that for many employees in an hotel the control test would in fact be sufficient to determine the issue. The jobs of porters, reception staff, reservation staff, kitchen and restaurant staff, chambermaids and maintenance staff are not so technically advanced that the hotelkeeper could not direct how they did their jobs.

(ii) The integration test

In *Stevenson, Jordan and Harrison Ltd v MacDonald and Evans*[208] Lord Denning said:

> "It is often easy to recognise a contract of service when you see it, but difficult to say wherein the difference lies. A ship's master, a chauffeur, and a reporter on the staff of a newspaper are all employed under a contract of service; but a ship's pilot, a taxi-man, and a newspaper, contributor

---

208 *[1952] 1 TLR 101*

are employed under a contract for services. One feature which seems to run through the instances is that, under a contract of service, a man is employed as part of the business, and his work is done as an integral part of the business; whereas, under a contract for services, his work, although done for the business, in not integrated into it but is only accessory to it."

The more fully integrated into the business the more likely a worker is to be regarded as an employee. Thus the driver of the hotel minibus which collects guests from the airport or the station, who wears the company uniform and is paid a weekly wage is an employee whereas the taxi driver who does the same job is not.

But there are more complicated examples. Let us say for the sake of argument that a small hotel has contracted its electrical work to an electrician who is in business on his own account and who is available 'on call' whenever required. As the business expands the hotel needs so much work from the electrician that it effectively becomes his exclusive employer. In recognition of this the hotel provides the electrician with an hotel uniform and allows him to eat in the staff canteen. However, he provides his own tools and decides his own hours. Has he crossed the border from independent contractor to employee? The answer to this probably cannot be answered by the integration test. Something more sophisticated is required.

(iii) The multiple test

In *Ready Mixed Concrete (South East), Ltd v Minister Of Pensions and National Insurance*[209] the facts of the case showed a high degree of integration yet ultimately the worker involved was held to be an independent contractor. It involved the owner-driver of a cement mixing lorry. Under a 30 page contract with RMC the driver was employed to deliver concrete. He purchased his lorry from the company and painted it in company colours and wore the company's uniform. The lorry had to be made exclusively available to the

---

209 *[1968] 2 QB 497*

company but he could employ suitable substitutes. He had to maintain the lorry at his own expense but the company insured it. The contract described him as an independent contractor.

McKenna J said:

> "A contract of service exists if the following three conditions are fulfilled: (i) The servant agrees that in consideration of a wage or other remuneration he will provide his own work and skill in the performance of some service for his master. (ii) He agrees, expressly or impliedly, that in the performance of that service he will be subject to the other's control in a sufficient degree to make that other master. (iii) The other provisions of the contract are consistent with its being a contract of service. I need say little about (i) and (ii)."

Applying this threefold test and coming to the conclusion that the driver was an independent contractor he stressed the entrepreneurial nature of the employment:

> "I have shown earlier that Mr. Latimer [the driver] must make the vehicle available throughout the contract period. He must maintain it (and also the mixing unit) in working order, repairing and replacing worn parts when necessary. He must hire a competent driver to take his place if he should be for any reason unable to drive at any time when the company requires the services of the vehicle. He must do whatever is needed to make the vehicle (with a driver) available throughout the contract period. He must do all this, at his own expense, being paid a rate per mile for the quantity which he delivers. These are obligations more consistent, I think, with a contract of carriage than with one of service. The ownership of the assets, the chance of profit and the risk of loss in the business of carriage are his and not the company's.

> If (as I assume) it must be shown that he has freedom

enough in the performance of those obligations to qualify as an independent contractor, I would say that he has enough. He is free to decide whether he will maintain the vehicle by his own labour or that of another, and, if he decides to use another's, he is free to choose whom he will employ and on what terms. He is free to use another's services to drive the vehicle when he is away because of sickness or holidays, or indeed at any other time when he has not been directed to drive himself. He is free again in his choice of a competent driver to take his place at these times, and whoever he appoints will be his servant and not the company's. He is free to choose where he will buy his fuel or any other of his requirements, subject to the company's control in the case of major repairs. This is enough. It is true that the company are given special powers to ensure that he runs his business efficiently, keeps proper accounts and pays his bills. I find nothing in these or any other provisions of the contract inconsistent with the company's contention that he is running a business of his own. A man does not cease to run a business on his own account because he agrees to run it efficiently or to accept another's superintendence."

Applying this case to the hotel electrician the decision would probably be that he remained an independent contractor, in business on his own account even though in a small way and with only one client.

(iv) Casual Workers

The hotel industry, being seasonal in nature, is known for employing numbers of casual workers. Are such workers employees? This issue arose in the case of *O'Kelly v Trusthouse Forte PLC*[210] the facts of which were that at the Grosvenor House Hotel, Trusthouse Forte carried on two distinct operations. They operated an hotel and a restaurant business which was open to the public, and by reason of the regular and continuous nature of that business the staff engaged were

210 *[1984] Q.B. 90 (CA)*

all employees working under contracts of employment. The company also carried on the business of hiring out rooms for private functions for which they provided the catering and other services. This part of the business was undertaken by the banqueting department. Because of the fluctuating and seasonal nature of this trade there were only 34 permanent staff. All the other staff in the department were known as casual staff and they were paid at a set rate for the work actually performed.

Because of the large number of casual staff required during the busy season and the difficulty of finding staff in sufficient numbers during the slack season a list of some 44 wine butlers and 60 food service waiters and waitresses was maintained. They were known as 'regulars' and were rostered in preference to other casual staff, numbering between 200 and 300, who worked less regularly and were employed for fewer functions. The 'regulars' were members of staff who could be relied upon by the company to offer their services regularly and, in return, had the assurance of preference in the allocation of any available work. They received exactly the same rate of remuneration as other casuals, but had the ability to earn more money by being offered more frequent engagements, and there was more regularity in their earnings. Because of the extent to which they made their services available to the company some 'regulars,' including the applicants, had no other regular employment.

The company chose to dismiss these 'regulars', who applied to an Employment Tribunal to have the dismissal declared unfair. Such a decision could only be taken if the regulars were employees rather than independent contractors. The Tribunal held that they were not employees on the grounds that although the relationship of the company to the applicants had many of the characteristics of a contract of service, the one important ingredient of mutuality of obligation was missing and that the applicants were in business on their own account as independent contractors supplying services and were not employees.

The Employment Appeal Tribunal overturned the decision, saying that these workers were employed on a series of short term contracts of employment but the Court of Appeal reinstated the decision of the Tribunal. The decision as to their status was a question of fact which the Court could not overturn unless the Tribunal had misdirected itself or no reasonable Tribunal could have come to that decision.

The decision has attracted criticism for notionally applying an economic reality test but in fact ignoring the substance of that test in that the workers provided no capital or equipment, there was no share in the profits, there was no use of agents and the hotel provided the uniforms.[211]

One way of understanding the decision is to realise that the context in which the question is being asked may be important. Many of the decisions relating to the distinction between employees and independent contractors have nothing to do with the vicarious liability of an employer for an employee's tort. Many of them are concerned with tax and national insurance matters where the issues are very different. The *Ready Mixed* case referred to above is a case in point. The issue in that case was who was responsible for paying national insurance contributions. In the *O'Kelly* case the workers had been dismissed for union activity. One can only speculate about the outcome of the case if the issue had been a question of tortious liability. Let's say for the sake of argument that one of the regulars had been serving hot soup and had spilled it over an hotel guest who was badly scalded as a result. In those circumstances one could easily see a court coming to the conclusion that the regular was an employee, albeit temporary.

(v) Agency workers

What if the hotel hires temporary staff from an employment agency? Are such staff employees of the hotel? The answer to this until recently was generally no but in the case of *Motorola Ltd v Davidson*[212] the Employment Appeal Tribunal held that an agency worker who had worked for a client for two years was an employee. The decision was based upon the control test and was made despite the fact that the

---

211 *For comment see Labour Law, Honeyball & Bowers, 7th ed., 2002 p.32*
212 *[2001] IRLR 4*

worker also had a legal relationship with the agency. A similar decision was reached in *Franks v Reuters Ltd*,[213] that a worker who had been employed by an agency client for six years *could* be classified as an employee. Mummery LJ stated that longevity of employment could be *capable* of establishing that a contract of employment had come into existence. Thus an hotel that employs staff through an agency could potentially find themselves liable for the tortious acts of the agency worker.

In the course of employment

Once it has been established that the tort was committed by an employee it must then be determined whether this was done in the course of the employee's employment, or, to use the time hallowed phrase, was he on a 'frolic of his own'?

In one sense, unless the employer authorises it, no tort is committed in the course of employment, simply because the employee is not employed to commit torts. But that is not how the law is applied. This is the classic test:

> "A master is not responsible for a wrongful act done by his servant unless it is done in the course of his employment. It is deemed to be so done if it is either (1) a wrongful act authorised by the master, or (2) a wrongful and unauthorised mode of doing some act authorised by the master."[214]

This test has been applied in numerous cases involving tortious acts by employees and is generally unexceptionable. In an hotel context the waiter that spills the hot soup over the dinner guest; the porter that drops and damages the guest's luggage; the minibus driver collecting the guest from the airport who negligently collides with another vehicle; the chef who causes food poisoning by undercooking the chicken and the laundry staff who burn the guest's shirt whilst ironing it are all committing torts in the course of their employment and their

---

213 *[2003] EWCA Civ 417*
214 *Salmond and Heuston on the Law of Torts, 21st ed., 1996*

employers would be liable. However there are circumstances which give rise to more difficulty.

What if the chambermaid steals from a guest's bedroom or the bar staff assault a customer? Are these actions committed in the course of employment? To take the example of theft first. The chambermaid has been given the *opportunity*, by her employment, to steal the property, but was this done in the course of her employment? Probably not. In the case of *Heasmans v Clarity Cleaning Company Ltd*[215] an employer was found not liable when a cleaner employed by them made unauthorised use of a client's telephone. Using the telephone was not an unauthorised mode of cleaning the telephone; it was not what she was employed to do at all. But this does not mean that all criminal acts are outside the course of employment. Take the case of *Lloyd v Grace, Smith & Co*,[216] a House of Lords case that held the employer, a firm of solicitors, liable when a clerk fraudulently deceived a client into transferring a mortgage into the clerk's name and then stole the mortgage money. The basis of liability was that the firm had held the clerk out as having the authority to perform that type of transaction. On that basis the desk clerk who fraudulently diverts money from a guest's credit card to his or her own account may very well make their employer vicariously liable.

The second example, an assault by staff, has been the subject of litigation in at least three common law jurisdictions. In *Petersson v Royal Oak Hotel Ltd*[217] the barman of an hotel had the duty to refuse liquor to any one not fit to consume any more, to order any offending person off the premises, and to keep order in the bar, and, in case of trouble, to report the matter to, and seek the assistance of, the bar manager, and not to take the law into his own hands. The barman picked up a piece of a broken glass thrown at him by a departing drunken customer to whom he had refused further drink, and throwing it at the latter, injured another customer who subsequently

---

215 *[1987] IRLR 286*
216 *[1912] AC 716*
217 *[1948] NZLR 136*

sued the owner of the hotel for damages. O'Leary CJ gave the following reasons for deciding that the act occurred in the course of the barman's employment:

> "As finally the decision depends on the particular facts, the first consideration is the ascertainment of what the barman was employed to do. 1 find from the evidence that, apart from the primary duty of serving customers, it was the duty of the barman to refuse liquor to anyone not fit to consume any more, to order any offending person off the premises, generally to keep order in the bar, and, in case of trouble, to report the matter to, and seek the assistance of the bar-manager. These words "to keep order" were not expressly used by any witness, but they are implicit in the evidence given by the licensee and the bar manager. The facts of the actual happening have already been set out at the commencement of this judgment, and there has never been any conflict between the parties as to what happened.

> On these findings as to the barman's work, I think there is little difficulty in arriving at an answer to the question of the master's liability.

> It was within the scope of Price's employment to keep order in the bar and to prevent altercations, and it was his duty to do that work with due and proper care so as to prevent injury or damage being occasioned to others. Quite apart from the question whether the throwing of the glass was an expression of Price's personal resentment at the glass having been thrown at him (and this matter I will deal with later), it is clear that, whatever his motive was, to throw the glass was not performing his work of keeping order, and preventing injury or damage, with the due and proper care which was demanded. It might be said that, as the customer was going out, no further action on the part of the barman was necessary, and, therefore, the act which caused the damage was independent of, and not connected

with, the employment. It is still the fact, however, that he performed the work of keeping order in a manner which was negligent, and, indeed, improper, and, instead of reducing the possibility of disorder, he contributed to it. It cannot be said, therefore, that what he did was an independent act unconnected with his employment; it was a personal act, but it was at the same time an improper mode of doing his work.

Apart from the application of the principles which I have cited from Salmond, I think the position is precisely covered by the statement by Lord Wright in *Century Insurance Co Ltd. v Northern Ireland Road Transport Board*[218] and quoted by the trial Judge as follows:

'The duty of the workman to his employer is so to conduct himself in doing his work as not negligently to cause damage either to the employer himself or his property or to third persons or their property, and thus to impose the same liability on the employer as if he had been doing the work himself and committed the negligent act. This may seem too obvious as a matter of common sense to require either arguments or authority. I think what plausibility the contrary argument might seem to possess results from treating the act of lighting the cigarette in abstraction from the circumstances as a separate act. This was the line taken by the majority judgment in *Williams v Jones* (1865) 3 H & C 602 but Mellor and Blackburn, JJ, dissented, rightly as I think.'

Mr. Cleary strongly argued that, as it had been found that the throwing of the glass was an expression of the barman's resentment, and not in order to expedite the departure of the troublesome customer, it was an

---

218 *[1942] AC 509*

independent act for which the employer was not liable. I am not disposed wholly to accept this finding. I think it might well be the case. that there was a double purpose, an expression of resentment and a desire to hurry the customer out. This would seem to be justified by the fact that the use of the words "Get to hell out of this" were used almost contemporaneously with the throwing, whilst the words "No one can throw a glass at me and get away with it" must have been used immediately afterwards. But, assuming it was resentment and nothing else, I still think liability exists. In the *Century* case the smoking and lighting of the cigarette was for the servants own pleasure, yet the master was liable because the servants act was a wrongful mode of doing his work. In the present case, even if it was because of resentment alone, the throwing of the glass was nevertheless a wrongful mode of keeping order, and liability is imposed on the employer."

On slightly different facts the court in *Griggs v Southside Hotel Ltd & German*[219] came to a different conclusion. In that case a waiter in a beer parlour had an argument with a customer about whether the customer would have to leave because he was drunk. In the course of the argument the customer became abusive and insulting to the waiter who responded by hitting the customer over the head with a beer bottle. It was held that the waiter was not acting in the course of his employment because the act of striking the customer was not connected with the act of removing the customer from the beer parlour. It was an independent act which had no relation to the business of the employer at the time it was done.

A third such case is *Vasey v Surrey Free Inns Plc*[220]. In that case the plaintiff had been refused admission to the defendants' nightclub. In a temper, he had kicked the door of the club and damaged the glass in it. He and his friends then left the premises. They were pursued by three

---

219 *[1947] 4 DLR 49*
220 *[1996] PIQR 373*

members of the defendants' staff: a manager and two doormen. One of the doormen struck the plaintiff on the head with a weapon, causing serious injury. The defendants' other two employees were holding the plaintiff at the time. The employees were authorised by the defendants to use physical force, if necessary, to protect the defendants' property. The plaintiff sought damages from the defendants on the ground of vicarious liability for the acts of their employees. The county court judge dismissed the claim and on appeal the decision was overturned. Ward LJ had this to say:

"The caricature of the bouncer at the disco door would show a gentleman of intimidating physical presence and menacing mien. Like all caricatures, it is revealing of an underlying reality which is that there is an expectation of violent confrontation with which the doorman is expected to cope. In a general sense, the job at which the defendants' employees were engaged was to control entry to the premises, to protect from harm both the premises themselves and also those persons employed there or peaceably enjoying its hospitality, to identify and, if and when necessary, to restrain the undesirable and unruly by reasonable force. Implicit therein was a discretion given to them as to whether and if so when to use force and as to the degree of force which was judged to be appropriate to contain the disturbance. Within that wide sphere of activity, an improper mode of carrying out that employment would include the use of unreasonable force exceeding the bounds of legitimate defence to person and property, and a measure of hot pursuit to confront the offender. When the plaintiff kicked at the door, the raiding party set out in such hot pursuit. Their purpose was made clear by their immediate enquiry of the group they had chased, as to the identity of whomsoever had caused the damage. They were clearly about their master's business. There was no evidence of their seeking redress for any personal injury or contumely suffered by any one of them in the exchanges which had taken place when the plaintiff and his friends had been earlier refused entry. There was no personal vendetta. The plaintiff, who had retreated into the car, was pulled out from it and beaten as has been described. This was not done just for the sake of a fight. The probability is overwhelming that the purpose of the beating was to exact retribution for the damage done to the club premises and by teaching the group a lesson and making of them an example of the bouncers' authority, to serve the general purpose of deterrence for the sake, however mistaken it was, of good order at the club.

It was, in my judgment, an unauthorised act which was within the province of their proper duty generally to preserve the integrity of the club. I adopt the test of Comyn J. in *Harrison v Michelin Tyre Co. Ltd*[221] and ask: "Was this incident so divergent from the employment as to be plainly alien to and distinguishable from it?" To that, on the facts of this case, I answer "No". This was not a frolic of their own, but an act for which the employer must be held vicariously liable."

Finally there is the case of *Daniels v Whetstone Entertainments Ltd*[222] where the claimant had been assaulted by a steward at a dance hall who had been employed to keep order and eject unruly patrons. There were in fact two assaults, the first as the claimant was being ejected and the second some time later outside the dance hall which was described as an act of vengeance by the steward who was retaliating for what he wrongfully thought has been an attack upon him by the claimant as he was being ejected. The first of the assaults was held to be in the course of his employment but the latter was not. Davies LJ said:

"Those being the principles, what are the essential facts of this case? Allender [the steward] was authorised to evict disorderly persons by the use of force, and forcibly to

---

221 [1985] 1 ICR 696
222 [1962] 2 Lloyds Rep 1

prevent their return. This does not, of course, mean that his authority to act terminated at the threshold. Obviously there might be cases where the actual act of eviction or the prevention of re-entry would involve the use of force in the street. Indeed, Mr. Bostock [the manager of the dance hall] in evidence said that he would not disapprove of a final shot outside to speed the parting guest or discourage any attempt on his part to return. But, subject to that, once the plaintiff had left and was showing no inclination to return, Allender was *functus officio.* The manager, after the plaintiff had left, gave Allender express instructions to return to the ballroom, and tried to lead him back. Those instructions Allender contumaciously repudiated. He then attempted to hit Metcalfe, and for a short distance pursued him. On Allender's return the plaintiff was chatting peacefully to this lady acquaintance, and making no attempt and showing no desire to return to the ballroom, or of showing any violence to Allender. Allender then assaulted the plaintiff as an act of private retaliation. In these circumstances I think there was a complete break between Allender's authorized province of operation and the subsequent events."

Lister v Hesley Hall Ltd

An important recent decision on what amounts to course of employment is the case of *Lister v Hesley Hall Ltd*[223] where the warden of a boys home sexually assaulted the boys in his care. The House of Lords adopted a broad approach to what is meant by course of employment. After reviewing the case law Lord Steyn said:

" ... it is not necessary to ask the simplistic question whether in the cases under consideration the acts of sexual abuse were modes of doing authorised acts. It becomes possible to consider the question of vicarious liability on the basis that the employer undertook to care for the boys

223 *[2002] 1 AC 215; [2001] UKHL 22.*

through the services of the warden and that there is a very *close connection* between the torts of the warden and his employment. After all, they were committed in the time and on the premises of the employers while the warden was also busy caring for the children." [Emphasis added]

And he went on to conclude:

"The question is whether the warden's torts were so closely connected with his employment that it would be fair and just to hold the employers vicariously liable. On the facts of the case the answer is yes. After all, the sexual abuse was inextricably interwoven with the carrying out by the warden of his duties in Axeholme House."

The reasoning in this case was adopted in *Mattis v Gerard Pollock (t/a Flamingo's Nightclub)*[224] another assault case involving a bouncer. In this case, which bears a remarkable similarity to the *Daniels* case referred to previously, a doorman of a club had assaulted some of the patrons, who had then turned on him and forced him to run off. He later returned with a knife and stabbed the claimant as an act of revenge for the humiliation he had suffered. Judge LJ gave the judgment of the court. In applying the *Lister* case he said:

"The essential principle we derive from the reasoning in *Lister* ... is that Mr Pollock's [the owner of the club] vicarious liability to Mr Mattis for Cranston's [the doorman] attack requires a deceptively simple question to be answered. Approaching the matter broadly, was the assault "so closely connected" with what Mr Pollock authorised or expected of Cranston in the performance of his employment as doorman at his nightclub, that it would be fair and just to conclude that Mr Pollock is vicariously liable for the damage Mr Mattis sustained when Cranston stabbed him."

The answer he came to was that:

---

224 *[2004] PIQR 3 (CA)*

"The stabbing of Mr Mattis represented the unfortunate, and virtual culmination of the unpleasant incident which had started within the club, and could not fairly and justly be treated in isolation from earlier events, or as a separate and distinct incident. Even allowing that Cranston's behaviour included an important element of personal revenge, approaching the matter broadly, at the moment when Mr Mattis was stabbed, the responsibility of Mr Pollock for the actions of his aggressive doorman was not extinguished. Vicarious liability was therefore established. Accordingly the appeal on this ground must succeed."

What distinguished this case from the *Daniels* case was that the owner of the club in the this case positively encouraged the aggressive behaviour of the doorman:

"Cranston was indeed employed by Mr Pollock to keep order and discipline at the nightclub. That is what bouncers are employed to do. Moreover, however, he was encouraged and expected to perform his duties in an aggressive and intimidatory manner, which included physical man-handling of customers ... Whether, taking Cranston's behaviour as a whole, it would have been appropriate to dismiss him, is a moot point. The reality was that Mr Pollock should not have been employing Cranston at all, and certainly should not have been encouraging him to perform his duties as he did. It was not perhaps anticipated that Cranston's behaviour would be counter-productive, and that by way of self-defence, and indeed revenge, his behaviour would provoke a violent response. That is because the customers with whom he tangled were supposed to be intimidated, and to go quietly. The whole point of any physical confrontation with Mr Pollock's customers in the nightclub, whether engineered by Cranston or not, was that he should win it."

Liability in Contract

Apart from his tortious liability the hotelkeeper also has duties in contract, under the Sale of Goods Act 1979 and the Supply of Goods and Services Act 1982.

Under this legislation we are essentially talking about the hotelkeeper's liability for the quality of the food he sells in his restaurants, or to put it more bluntly, his liability for guests who become ill after consuming the food. Other aspects of food quality such as its presentation and its quantity are not matters of health and safety and are not the subject of discussion.

As indicated, the hotelkeeper might have liability under the Sale of Goods Act 1979 (SGA) or the Supply of Goods and Services Act 1982 (SOGSA). The former covers straightforward sales of goods whereas the latter covers a number of situations including those where both goods and services are sold. Thus meals served by an hotel in a restaurant offering waiter service would be a contract for goods and services[225] whereas the guest who consumed the drink and snacks from the fridge in his room, or who purchased soft drinks or confectionery from the vending machine in the corridor, would have a sale of goods contract. A purchase of a scone and a cup of tea in the hotel's cafeteria is also, almost certainly, a sale of goods contract.

It used to be the case that distinguishing between the two types of contract was of crucial importance because the duties placed upon the seller of goods as opposed to a supplier of goods and services were different. The issue was whether or not the seller was strictly liable for the goods supplied or only liable to exercise reasonable care and skill in their supply. In the context of hotel meals does the hotelier guarantee the quality of the food or does he merely promise that he will exercise care and skill in its preparation and will not be liable for any latent defects which reasonable care would not have revealed?

Today, fortunately, this problem does not arise in an hotel context largely because the duties under SOGSA are identical or very similar to

---

225 But see *Lockett v Charles [1938] 4 All ER 170 discussed below.*

the duties under the SGA. However, legally speaking, the two kinds of contract are distinct and the hotelkeeper's duties certainly arise from two different sources, and they need separate treatment. However before looking at the law in more detail we shall set out the relevant statutory provisions. Broadly speaking the duties are threefold:

- To supply goods which comply with their description
- To supply goods which are of satisfactory quality
- To supply goods which are fit for a particular purpose made known to the seller

Although the duties are distinct there is often some overlap between them. To serve food described as 'fresh' when in fact it is rotten would offend against both the duty to provide food which complies with its description as well as the duty to provide food of satisfactory quality.

Sale of Goods Act. The duty to provide goods of the right description.

Section 13 of the Sale of Goods Act provides:

> 13(1) Where there is a contract for the sale of goods by description, there is an implied term that the goods will correspond with the description.

Sale of Goods Act. The duty to provide goods of satisfactory quality.

Section 14 of the Sale of Goods Act provides:

> 14(1) Except as provided by this section and section 15 below and subject to any other enactment, there is no implied term about the quality or fitness for any particular purpose of goods supplied under a contract of sale.
>
> (2) Where the seller sells goods in the course of a business, there is an implied term that the goods supplied under the contract are of satisfactory quality.
>
> (2A) For the purposes of this Act, goods are of satisfactory quality if they meet the standard that a reasonable

person would regard as satisfactory, taking account of any description of the goods, the price (if relevant) and all the other relevant circumstances.

(2B) For the purposes of this Act, the quality of goods includes their state and condition and the following (among others) are in appropriate cases aspects of the quality of goods–

(a) fitness for all the purposes for which goods of the kind in question are commonly supplied,

(b) appearance and finish,

(c) freedom from minor defects,

(d) safety, and

(e) durability.

(2C) The term implied by subsection (2) above does not extend to any matter making the quality of goods unsatisfactory–

(a) which is specifically drawn to the buyer's attention before the contract is made,

(b) where the buyer examines the goods before the contract is made, which that examination ought to reveal, or

(c) in the case of a contract for sale by sample, which would have been apparent on a reasonable examination of the sample.

...

(3) Where the seller sells goods in the course of a business and the buyer, expressly or by implication, makes known–

(a) to the seller ...

(b) ... any particular purpose for which the goods are being bought, there is an implied term that the goods supplied under the contract are reasonably fit for that purpose, whether or not that is a purpose for which such goods are commonly supplied, except where the circumstances show that the buyer does not rely, or that it is unreasonable for him to rely, on the skill or judgment of the seller or credit-broker.

Supply of Goods and Services Act. The duty to provide goods of the right description.

Section 3 of SOGSA provides:

3(1) This section applies where, under a contract for the transfer of goods, the transferor transfers or agrees to transfer the property in the goods by description.

(2) In such a case there is an implied condition that the goods will correspond with the description.

Supply of Goods and Services Act. The duty to provide goods of satisfactory quality.

Section 4 of SOGSA provides:

4(1) Except as provided by this section and section 5 below and subject to the provisions of any other enactment, there is no implied condition or warranty about the quality or fitness for any particular purpose of goods supplied under a contract for the transfer of goods.

(2) Where, under such a contract, the transferor transfers the property in goods in the course of a business, there is an implied condition that the goods supplied under the contract are of satisfactory quality.

(2A)   For the purposes of this section and section 5 below, goods are of satisfactory quality if they meet the standard that a reasonable person would regard as satisfactory, taking account of any description of the goods, the price (if relevant) and all the other relevant circumstances.

(3)   The condition implied by subsection (2) above does not extend to any matter making the quality of goods unsatisfactory–

(a) which is specifically drawn to the transferee's attention before the contract is made,

(b) where the transferee examines the goods before the contract is made, which that examination ought to reveal, or

(c) where the property in the goods is transferred by reference to a sample, which would have been apparent on a reasonable examination of the sample.

The right description

An hotel might have a restaurant famous for its seafood which it advertises on the menu as 'bought fresh every morning from the fish market'. If, as indicated above, the fish was rotten and caused food poisoning there would almost certainly be a case under both s.13 SGA and s.3 SOGSA for a breach of the implied term that the goods would correspond with their description.

Where the food is not displayed and the guest's choice is from a menu, or on the basis of a recommendation from one of the serving staff, it is difficult to see how this would ever be other than a sale *by description*. In *Varley v Whip*[226] the court said that the provision

"must apply to all cases where the purchaser has not seen the goods but is relying on the description alone."

---

226 *[1900] 1 QB 513*

Of course liability would depend upon the nature of the description. It may be that the guest has an allergy to nuts and specifically enquires whether or not the food contains nuts. If an assurance were given that there were no nuts in the food but in fact there were the guest could sue on the basis of the false description. However if both the menu and the waiter were silent as to the presence of nuts then there would be no liability as there was no misdescription of the food. The same considerations would apply where the guest was concerned about whether the food was gluten free.

Note that in these circumstances an action under s.3 SOGSA, or s.13 SGA for breach of the term relating to description would be superior to an action under s.4 or s.14 respectively because in these cases the food would, in most cases, be regarded as of satisfactory quality.

If the food is displayed, say at a breakfast buffet, for the guest to choose their own food would this be a sale by description? One's initial reaction is perhaps to say no, the guest is selecting his own food from what is in front of him, but case law suggests otherwise. The leading case is *Grant v Australian Knitting Mills*[227] where the buyer purchased some woollen underwear contaminated by chemicals which caused an extreme allergic reaction. On the issue of whether the goods had been bought by description the court had this to say:

> "It may also be pointed out that there is a sale by description even though the buyer is buying something displayed before him on the counter: a thing is sold by description, though it is specific, so long as it is sold not merely as the specific thing but as a thing corresponding to a description, e.g. woollen under-garments, a hot-water bottle, a second-hand reaping machine, to select a few obvious illustrations." [Lord Wright][228]

---

227 *[1936] AC 85*

228 *The authors of 'Sale of Goods', Atiyah, Adams & MacQueen, 10th ed., 2001, point out that this list appears somewhat surreal to a non-lawyer. It makes sense only to lawyers who know that it is derived from decided cases.*

Thus the items on the breakfast buffet could be sold by description – if there were any description applied to them. Simply displaying the sausages or rashers of bacon would not amount to a sale by description. However if the ingredients of the food were listed then it could be a sale by description.

Wren v Holt[229] is a Court of Appeal case decided under the Sale of Goods Act 1893 where the provisions were different from the current Act. The facts of the case were that the plaintiff had bought a pint of Holden's beer in a beerhouse and the beer had been contaminated by arsenic. To establish his case he had to show that the beer had been bought by description. If he could establish that then the Act implied a warranty as to the quality of the goods. On this issue, agreeing with the decision of the jury, Stirling LJ said:

> "The plaintiff was in the habit of going to the house because there he could get Holden's beer, and, upon the facts found by the jury, he in substance bought by that description."

Satisfactory Quality

S.4 SOGSA and s.14 SGA provide that goods must be of satisfactory quality. *Lockett v Charles*, referred to earlier is a clear example of a case falling within this provision. The facts were that the plaintiffs, who were husband and wife, stopped for lunch at a hotel owned by the defendant company. The meal included whitebait, and the female plaintiff, having swallowed a mouthful of the whitebait, refused to eat the remainder. She was subsequently taken ill, and it was contended that the illness was due to the fact that the food supplied was unfit for human consumption. It was argued that there was a breach of an implied term of the contract under which the meal was supplied.

The main issue in the case was whether the female plaintiff had privity of contract with the defendant but once that issue was settled in her favour the court had no problem holding the defendant liable for the unsatisfactory food.

229 *[1903] 1 KB 610*

Interestingly the purchase of the meal was treated, without argument, as a sale of goods rather than a contract for goods and services. Presumably the rationale for this is that the food was the *substance* of the contract rather than the service.[230]

Another interesting feature of the case is that originally the plaintiff had tried to prove negligence on the part of the defendant but had abandoned that line of attack in favour of the contractual claim – demonstrating the advantage that the strict liability contractual action has over the fault based claim in tort. Had the facts been slightly different Mrs Lockett might have found herself in the same position as the famous plaintiff in *Donoghue v Stevenson*,[231] of having to sue the defendant in tort because there was no one with whom she had a contract.

Both Acts have provisos to the effect that if the buyer had examined the goods and the examination ought to have revealed the defect that makes the goods unsatisfactory, or if the seller had pointed out the defect, the warranty of satisfactory quality would not apply. One can imagine a guest ordering afternoon tea in the foyer of an hotel and when it arrives, suspects that the milk for the tea might be a little 'off', but rather than complaining chooses to use the milk but then becomes ill. On the face of it this might be an example of the first proviso in action but this would not be so. Both provisos only apply if the examination or the warning takes place 'before the contract is made'. So in our example the goods are already of unsatisfactory quality before the contract is made and the hotel cannot invoke the legislation to protect itself.

Nevertheless the hotel could defend itself on grounds of causation. What was the cause of the guest's illness – the fact that the milk was sour or the fact that the guest chose to drink it in the knowledge that it was not fresh? It would seem that the actions of the guest would be enough to break the chain of causation, thus relieving the hotel of liability. At the very least the hotel could claim contributory negligence.

---

230 *Robinson v Graves [1935] 1 KB 579*
231 *[1932] AC 562*

Fit for a particular purpose

As well as the general requirement that goods have to be of satisfactory quality there is the additional requirement that if they are sold for a *particular purpose*, whether or not that is a purpose for which goods of that kind are usually supplied, the goods must be fit for *that purpose*. For example, a parent might order food for a young child and specifically state that the food was not to be too hot in case the child burnt its mouth. If, in contravention of these instructions, the food turned out to be too hot and the child was burnt then there would be an action against the hotel – even though the food might have been perfectly satisfactory for an adult.[232]

Earlier it was said that there was an overlap between the implied terms in s.3 SOGSA and s.13 SGA relating to description, and the implied terms in s.4 SOGSA and s.14 SGA relating to quality. This can be clearly illustrated by the example of the guest with an allergy to nuts. If the hotel provides food with nuts in it after a guest has specifically requested otherwise this will be a breach of the implied term about description (s.3 and s.13). It will also be a breach of the requirement to provide food of satisfactory quality – the definition of takes into account 'any description of the goods'. Finally there would be a breach of the requirement to provide goods for a particular purpose i.e. for someone who has a nut allergy.

Privity of Contract

In the case of *Lockett v Charles* discussed earlier the principal issue was not really whether the food was unsatisfactory but whether the female plaintiff had a contract with the hotel. That problem was solved by the court deciding she did:

"I think that the inference is that the person who orders the food in a hotel or restaurant *prima facie* makes himself or herself liable to pay for it, and when two people –

---

232 *Note however with this example that the child would have the same problem with privity of contract as the plaintiff in Lockett v Charles – subject to what is said later.*

whether or not they happen to be husband and wife – go into a hotel and each orders and is supplied with food, then, as between those persons and the proprietor of the hotel, each of them is making himself liable for the food which he orders, whatever may be the arrangement between the two persons who are eating at the hotel. On the facts in this case, it is, in my opinion, right to hold that there was a contract implied by the conduct of the parties between the plaintiff, Mrs Lockett, and the defendants when she ordered and was supplied with the whitebait at the Hotel de Paris." [Tucker J]

That approach would not however solve the problem of our infant burnt by the hot food. It would be hard to construct a contract, however hard one tried, between the infant and the hotel.[233] Fortunately this problem has largely been solved by the Contracts (Rights of Third Parties) Act 1999. Broadly speaking the Act provides that where someone has made a contract for the benefit of a third party that person is entitled to sue in their own right for breach of contract. Thus Mrs Locket would no longer have to argue that she had a contract in her own right, she could claim that she was a third party beneficiary.

The relevant provisions of the Act are as follows:

1(1) Subject to the provisions of this Act, a person who is not a party to a contract (a "third party") may in his own right enforce a term of the contract if–

(a) the contract expressly provides that he may, or

(b) subject to subsection (2), the term purports to confer a benefit on him.

(2) Subsection (1)(b) does not apply if on a proper construction of the contract it appears that the parties did not intend the term to be enforceable by the third party.

---

233 *See the remarks of Denning MR in Jackson v Horizon Holidays [1975] 1 WLR 1468 on this point.*

(3) The third party must be expressly identified in the contract by name, as a member of a class or as answering a particular description but need not be in existence when the contract is entered into.

Thus when Mr and Mrs Lockett walk into the restaurant and they both order food but Mr Lockett makes it clear that he will be paying Mrs Lockett may nevertheless sue in her own right on the basis that there is a term in the contract between the hotel and Mr Lockett which purports to confer a benefit on her (s.1(1)(b)) and she was expressly identified in the contract (s.1(3)). It would be the same for the infant and the hot food. The parent would have made a contract with the hotel for the benefit of the (infant) third party who could then sue in his own right.

It should be noted that the Act does not apply only in these circumstances, it has a much wider scope than the purchase of food from the hotel. It would extend to any situation where one person makes a booking on behalf of others, in particular the booking of rooms and other facilities.

Consumer Protection Act 1987

In this final section we shall examine the hotelkeeper's strict liability under the Consumer Protection Act 1987 (CPA).

This Act was passed in order to comply with our obligations to implement EC Directive on Liability for Defective Products (85/374/EEC). Broadly speaking the Act imposes liability on a range of defendants for the supply of 'defective' products. As already indicated, the Act, by imposing strict liability on defendants, does not require proof of fault by a claimant. This, combined with the fact that there is also no need to prove a contractual relationship, provides the claimant with advantages over both tortious and contractual actions.

We shall examine in turn who can sue and be sued, what is meant by a defective product and the defences available.

Claimants

The Act does not say in so many words who can bring an action but it is implicit in s.2 which provides:

> 2(1) Subject to the following provisions of this Part, where any damage is caused wholly or partly by a defect in a product, every person to whom subsection (2) below applies shall be liable for the damage.

Thus *any* person damaged by a defective product can bring an action against the persons specified in s.2(2). This is not limited by the rules of privity of contract that were examined in the last section. Thus the problems encountered by the plaintiff in *Lockett v Charles*[234] discussed previously would not arise with an action under the CPA. Whether Mrs Lockett had purchased the meal or not would not be an issue. If the hotel had served her a 'defective' meal they could be liable if they fell within the list of potential defendants.

Any person, whether an individual diner, a member of a family party or a group out for a Christmas lunch could all sue under the CPA irrespective of who made the booking or paid the bill.

Defendants

To determine who can be sued we need to look at s.2. This provides:

> 2(1) Subject to the following provisions of this Part, where any damage is caused wholly or partly by a defect in a product, every person to whom subsection (2) below applies shall be liable for the damage.
>
> (2) This subsection applies to—
>
> (a) the producer of the product;
>
> (b) any person who, by putting his name on the product or using a trade mark or other distinguishing mark in relation to the product, has held himself out to be the producer of the product;

---

234 *[1938] 4 All ER 170*

(c) any person who has imported the product into a member State from a place outside the member States in order, in the course of any business of his, to supply it to another.

(3) Subject as aforesaid, where any damage is caused wholly or partly by a defect in a product, any person who supplied the product (whether to the person who suffered the damage, to the producer of any product in which the product in question is comprised or to any other person) shall be liable for the damage if–

(a) the person who suffered the damage requests the supplier to identify one or more of the persons (whether still in existence or not) to whom subsection (2) above applies in relation to the product;

(b) that request is made within a reasonable period after the damage occurs and at a time when it is not reasonably practicable for the person making the request to identify all those persons; and

(c) the supplier fails, within a reasonable period after receiving the request, either to comply with the request or to identify the person who supplied the product to him.

Briefly, this section provides that the following persons can be defendants:

● Producers
● Those who hold themselves out as producers
● Importers
● In certain circumstances, the supplier of the product

Given the right circumstances hotelkeepers could fall into any of these categories.

(i) *Producers*

Producers are defined in s.1 in the following way:

> "producer", in relation to a product, means–
>
> (a) the person who manufactured it;
>
> (b) in the case of a substance which has not been manufactured but has been won or abstracted, the person who won or abstracted it;
>
> (c) in the case of a product which has not been manufactured, won or abstracted but essential characteristics of which are attributable to an industrial or other process having been carried out (for example, in relation to agricultural produce), the person who carried out that process;

Clearly (b) does not apply to an hotelkeeper serving food and it is arguable whether (a) does either. It would seem an abuse of the English language to say that the hotel 'manufactured' its meals. On the other hand what is the difference between an hotel serving hundreds of meals at a banquet and a small food processor producing a range of pre-packaged individual meals at its factory – apart from the fact that the former serves its food fresh and the latter does not?

As far as (c) is concerned it would seem that many of the meals served by an hotel would place it within this category. The hotel will buy in raw materials and then prepare them in such a way that their *essential characteristics* are attributable to an industrial or *other process* having been carried out on it. There is a world of difference between the raw ingredients that go into a 'Northumbrian Broth' and the final product – a bowl of hot nourishing soup. On the other hand the provision of a bowl of fresh fruit or perhaps a simple salad would not qualify the hotelkeeper as a processor no matter how artfully it was arranged because the essential characteristics are not due to that process. On the other hand in *B v McDonald's Restaurants Ltd*[235] the defendants

---

235 *[2002] EWHC 490*

accepted that simply adding hot water to coffee or tea made them producers.

(ii) Those who hold themselves out as producers

The prime target of this provision is those supermarkets who take the products of other manufacturers and affix their own-brand labels to it. It is difficult to see how this would apply to hotelkeepers. They are usually not in the habit of putting their own brand on the food they serve – largely because it would be otiose, the guests would usually never see the label anyway. However it may happen with wine. Some hotels put their own name on the wine that they serve. In such instances they may fall foul of the Act. However much may depend on the circumstances. If the label simply describes the wine as 'Grand Hotel Wine' with no qualifications on the label it would seem that they are holding themselves out as producers. On the other hand if the label goes on to say 'Grown and bottled for the Grand Hotel by California Wines Inc.' then can it is arguable that they are holding themselves out as producers? It may very well depend upon how prominent the name of the Grand Hotel is and how small the print is.

(iii) Importers

Again it is unlikely that an hotel would fall into this category largely because they would usually purchase their food in the UK or through a UK food importer. However it is not beyond the bounds of possibility, especially with the spread of the internet, that the hotel might order food direct from a supplier outside the EU. If they did that then they would be liable for any defects in the product. Note that importing from another country in the EU would not attract liability.

(iv) Suppliers

The effect of s.2(3) is that someone who merely supplies a product produced or imported by another is generally not liable for any defects in the product. So long as the supplier, in this case an hotel, can identify the producer, own-brander or importer, or who supplied the product to them then they will escape liability.

The danger here for hotels is that if they acquire produce from multiple suppliers and cannot identify the source of their supply they may find themselves liable. It is important that proper records are kept so that liability can be passed back up the distribution chain. Given that the hotelkeeper would now have to comply with the record keeping requirements imposed by food safety legislation[236] it would be largely their own fault if they could not identify their supplier.

Meaning of defective

The definition of a defective product is found in s.3:

3(1) Subject to the following provisions of this section, there is a defect in a product for the purposes of this Part if the safety of the product is not such as persons generally are entitled to expect; and for those purposes "safety", in relation to a product, shall include safety with respect to products comprised in that product and safety in the context of risks of damage to property, as well as in the context of risks of death or personal injury.

(2) In determining for the purposes of subsection (1) above what persons generally are entitled to expect in relation to a product all the circumstances shall be taken into account, including—

(a) the manner in which, and purposes for which, the product has been marketed, its get-up, the use of any mark in relation to the product and any instructions for, or warnings with respect to, doing or refraining from doing anything with or in relation to the product;

(b) what might reasonably be expected to be done with or in relation to the product; and

(c) the time when the product was supplied by its producer to another;

---

236 *Food Safety Act 1990 (Amendment) Regulations 2004 (SI 2004 No. 2990)*

and nothing in this section shall require a defect to be inferred from the fact alone that the safety of a product which is supplied after that time is greater than the safety of the product in question.

The essence of this definition is that the product, in our case the hotel food, is not as safe as guests can reasonably expect. Thus if the chicken is infected with salmonella or the fresh fruit is contaminated with toxic pesticides this would clearly be an infringement of the Act – as indeed it would be if the cold drink contained a decomposed snail.

Safety is of course a relative concept and what is generally regarded as safe will vary according to the circumstances. The legislation recognises this by indicating factors which may be taken into account when assessing the defectiveness of a product, such as labelling and warnings and how the product can be expected to be used. In *B v McDonald's* referred to earlier the issue was whether or not McDonald's served their coffee too hot – in the light of several accidents involving children who had been scalded when cups had been overturned. The judge held not:

"80. Persons generally expect tea or coffee purchased to be consumed on the premises to be hot. Many prefer to consume a hot drink from an unlidded cup rather than through a spout in the lid. Persons generally know that if a hot drink is spilled onto someone, a serious scalding injury can result. They accordingly know that care must be taken to avoid such spills, especially if they are with young children. They expect precautions to be taken to guard against this risk but not to the point that they are denied the basic utility of being able to buy hot drinks to be consumed on the premises from a cup with the lid off. Given that the staff were trained to cap the drinks securely and given the capabilities of the cups and lids used, I am satisfied that the safety of the hot drinks served by McDonald's was such as persons generally are entitled to expect. Accordingly, I hold that in serving hot drinks in the manner in which they did McDonald's was not in breach of the CPA."

A problem referred to previously is the issue of guests with allergies. What if the cake served by the hotel contains nuts and a guest allergic to nuts suffered a reaction to this? The issue here is that this particular guest has a specific condition that is not shared with most of the rest of the public. Should the hotel be liable to such persons? The Act itself refers to 'persons generally' which suggests that if the defect affects only a small section of the population then the product may not be regarded as defective.

Note however that the Directive does not refer to 'persons generally'. It provides that

> 'a product is defective when it does not provide the safety which *a person* is entitled to expect ...' [Emphasis added].

This is broader than the Act and suggests that if the individual consumer can show that he is entitled to expect the product to be free of nuts or to be warned of their presence then it is defective.

Currently the problem is regarded as sufficiently serious that there has now been statutory intervention as far as the labelling of food products is concerned[237] which requires the listing of certain allergens on the product (although this does not extend to meals sold in restaurants). Does this mean that the problem is sufficiently widespread that hotelkeepers serving such food should provide warnings?

And what of the person who takes more than he needs at the breakfast buffet so that he can have a snack later in his room. The bread bun and the cheese may survive relatively unharmed in his warm room but the cold meat may deteriorate rapidly. If this causes food poisoning is the hotelkeeper to be liable. If the guest chooses to remove the food from the dining room and consume it sometime later in adverse conditions is this something which 'might reasonably be expected to be done with or in relation to the product'? Presumably not.

---

237 *Food Labelling (Amendment)(No. 2) Regulations 2004 (SI 2824/2004)*

Defences

The defences are set out in s.4:

> 4(1) In any civil proceedings by virtue of this Part against any person ("the person proceeded against") in respect of a defect in a product it shall be a defence for him to show—
>
> > (a) that the defect is attributable to compliance with any requirement imposed by or under any enactment or with any Community obligation; or
> >
> > (b) that the person proceeded against did not at any time supply the product to another; or
> >
> > (c) that the following conditions are satisfied, that is to say—
> >
> > (i) that the only supply of the product to another by the person proceeded against was otherwise than in the course of a business of that person's; and
> >
> > (ii) that section 2(2) above does not apply to that person or applies to him by virtue only of things done otherwise than with a view to profit; or
> >
> > (d) that the defect did not exist in the product at the relevant time; or
> >
> > (e) that the state of scientific and technical knowledge at the relevant time was not such that a producer of products of the same description as the product in question might be expected to have discovered the defect if it had existed in his products while they were under his control; or
> >
> > (f) that the defect—
> >
> > (i) constituted a defect in a product ("the subsequent product") in which the product in question had been comprised; and

(ii) was wholly attributable to the design of the subsequent product or to compliance by the producer of the product in question with instructions given by the producer of the subsequent product.

(2) In this section "the relevant time", in relation to electricity, means the time at which it was generated, being a time before it was transmitted or distributed, and in relation to any other product, means—

(a) if the person proceeded against is a person to whom subsection (2) of section 2 above applies in relation to the product, the time when he supplied the product to another;

(b) if that subsection does not apply to that person in relation to the product, the time when the product was last supplied by a person to whom that subsection does apply in relation to the product

It is difficult to see how any of these defences might apply to an hotelkeeper serving food to guests. The example given above of the guest who removes the food from the breakfast buffet for consumption later may provide one example. Under s.4(1)(d) the defendant will escape liability if they can show that the defect did not exist at the 'relevant time'. Relevant time is defined in s.4(2)(a) as the time when, in our case, the hotelkeeper (if he is a producer) supplies it to the guest. If the food was not defective at the buffet then any subsequent deterioration will not affect his liability.

Initially it may appear that s.4(1)(b) might provide a defence. This applies where the defendant did not *supply* the product to the claimant. This provision is intended to cover, amongst other things, the theft of products. If a guest who had booked 'room only' simply helped himself, with no assistance from hotel staff, to the contents of the breakfast buffet i.e. he stole the food, and if some of it proved to be defective he would appear to have no cause of action. Contrast this however with the guest who brazenly presents himself at mealtime and fraudulently gives the maitre d' the name and room number of another guest and who is then seated and served a full meal. Has the hotel *supplied* the guest with the defective meal? If so then the hotel would appear to be liable.

However a closer look at s.4 rules this defence out even for the thief. The provision applies, not to the supply of the product to a particular claimant, but to supplying the product *at any time to another.* So once the defective food is placed on the buffet or on the menu for general consumption even the guest who steals cannot be met by the s.(4)(1)(b) defence.

This approach can be supported by looking at the Directive. The Directive does not use the word 'supply'. Instead the phrase used is whether the producer has 'put the product into circulation'. In our example once the food is set out on the breakfast buffet it has been *put into circulation* even though it may not have been *supplied*. In terms of reconciling the two, regard should be had to s.1 of the Act which states:

> S.1(1) This part shall have effect for the purpose of making such provision as is necessary in order to comply with the product liability Directive and shall be construed accordingly.

Faced with this situation the hotelkeeper might have to call upon the common law defence of *ex turpi causa non oritur actio* (illegality) but it is arguable whether even this would apply.

Other products

We have concentrated on the supply of food by the hotelkeeper but occasionally the hotelkeeper does supply other products, for instance the toiletries in the bathroom and the free pens at the bedside. Should these prove defective the hotelkeeper could also be liable. For instance the shampoo might contain the wrong balance of chemicals and cause a reaction when used or the plastic used in the manufacture of the pen might be too brittle and when the pen is used it might split and cut the guest. The principles applicable to the supply of food would apply equally to these other products, in particular was the hotelkeeper only a supplier or would they be primarily liable as an 'own-brander' if they affixed their own logo to these products.

Concurrent liability with contract and tort

It will have become apparent that an action under the CPA will often overlap with an action in contract or tort. Often such an action will not give the claimant any advantages over these other actions. Where the Act does give the claimant an advantage would be those circumstances, probably few in number, where there was no negligence by the hotelkeeper and where the guest had no contract with the hotel. This might apply where for instance the bowl of fruit in the guest's room or the snacks and drinks provided in the executive lounge were not supplied by virtue of a contract but provided as a complimentary service by the hotel. Should these turn out to be defective the guest would only have his rights under the CPA to fall back upon.

CHAPTER SIX
HOTELKEEPERS' LIABILITY FOR THE PROPERTY OF GUESTS

Introduction

In the last chapter we looked at an hotelkeeper's responsibility for the safety of his guests and we have seen that this is predominantly fault based – the law of negligence. We are now moving on to examine the hotelkeeper's responsibility for a guest's property and here we shall see that this liability is strict and its origins go back to the earliest cases on innkeeping law. We shall also see that this strict liability has been partially mitigated by statute, the Hotel Proprietors Act 1956, which permits hotelkeepers to limit their liability in certain circumstances.

The origins of the rule

Lord Macmillan, in *Shacklock v Ethorpe Ltd*,[238] provides an authoritative statement of the hotelkeeper's liability and its origins in some of our earliest case law:

> "By the common law of England, an innkeeper is responsible to his guests if any of their goods are lost or stolen while on his premises. As it was put so long ago as 1550 in argument in *Reniger v Fogossa*,[239] at p 9:
>
> ' ... by the common custom of the realm, hosts shall be charged for the goods of their guests lost or stolen out of their houses ...'

---

238 *[1939] 3 All ER 372*
239 *(1552) 1 Plowd 1.*

The principle, whose origin is discussed by Lord Esher, then Brett J in *Nugent v Smith*,[240] is common to most, if not all, systems of jurisprudence, and was first promulgated in the praetors' edict, nautae, caupones, stabularii.[241] It has been said historically to have arisen from the view that the goods of travellers were exposed to special risk owing to the danger of collusion between innkeepers and thieves.

... In the words of Lord Esher MR, in *Robins & Co v Gray*,[242] at pp 503, 504:

'The duties, liabilities, and rights of innkeepers with respect to goods brought to inns by guests are founded, not upon bailment, or pledge, or contract, but upon the custom of the realm with regard to innkeepers. Their rights and liabilities are dependent upon that, and that alone; they do not come under any other head of law ... the innkeeper's liability is not that of a bailee or pledgee of goods; he is bound to keep them safely. It signifies not, so far as that obligation is concerned if they are stolen by burglars, or by the servants of the inn, or by another guest; he is liable for not keeping them safely unless they are lost by the fault of the traveller himself. That is a tremendous liability: it is a liability fixed upon the innkeeper by the fact that he has taken the goods in ...'"

The matter is put a little more succinctly in an article in The Law Times[243] where the author states:

"The rule in *Calye's case*[244] may, we think, be stated fairly

---

240 *(1875) 1 CPD 19; 3 Digest 53, 2, 45 LJQB 19, 33 LT 731, revsd on another point (1876) 1 CPD 423*

241 *Shipmasters, innkeepers and stablekeepers.*

242 *[1895] 2 QB 501*

243 *The Law Times, Aug. 5, 1939, Volume 188 p.91 .*

244 *(1853) 8 Co. Rep. 32a; 77 ER 520*

by saying that if a man keeps an inn it is his business to keep thieves out of it, and the common law liability of the innkeeper, like that of the carrier, may well have been invented by the judges to circumvent the machinations of innkeepers who 'leagued themselves with thieves'."

Two American cases also give us the rationale for the strict rule:

"This custom, like the kindred case of the common carrier, had its origin in considerations of public policy. It was essential to the interests of the realm, that every facility should be furnished for secure and convenient intercourse between different portions of the kingdom. The safeguards, of which the law gave assurance to the wayfarer, were akin to those which invested each English home with the legal security of a castle. The traveller was peculiarly exposed to depredation and fraud. He was compelled to repose confidence in a host, who was subject to constant temptation, and favoured with peculiar opportunities, if he chose to betray his trust ... The care of the property was usually committed to servants, over whom the guest had no control, and who had no interest in its preservation, unless their employer was held responsible for its safety. In case of depredation by collusion, or of injury or destruction by neglect, the stranger would of necessity be at every possible disadvantage. He would be without the means either of proving guilt or detecting it ... The sufferer would be deprived, by the very wrong of which he complained, of the means of remaining to ascertain and enforce his rights, and redress would be well-nigh hopeless, but for the rule of law casting the loss on the party entrusted with the custody of the property, and paid for keeping it safely."[245]

"At common law an innkeeper was practically an insurer of the goods of a guest lost in the inn. With the exception of

---

245 *Hulett v Swift 33 NY 571*

a loss occurring by act of God or a public enemy or by the fault or negligence of the guest himself, the innkeeper was liable for the loss of a guest's property, however occurring. To recover, all the guest had to prove was that his property was lost while in the inn. It made no difference that the innkeeper may have used the greatest care to protect the guest's property. The innkeeper's liability was absolute to him other than the mentioned exceptions. No business, with the possible exception of common carriers, was more rigorously governed by common law than that of innkeepers.

The imposition of strict liability on the innkeeper found its origin in the conditions existing in England in the fourteenth and fifteenth centuries. Inadequate means of travel, the sparsely settled country and the constant exposure to robbers left the traveler with the inn practically his only hope for protection. Innkeepers themselves, and their servants, were often as dishonest as the highwaymen roaming the countryside and were not beyond joining forces with the outlaws to relieve travelers and guests, by connivance or force, of their valuables and goods. Under such conditions it was purely a matter of necessity and policy for the law to require the innkeeper to exert his utmost efforts to protect his guests' property and to assure results by imposing legal liability for loss without regard to fault."[246]

The extent of the rule

Although the rule is strict it is not absolute. In certain circumstances the innkeeper will not be liable for the loss of a guest's property. The first of these exceptions, and the only one of any real significance, is where the innkeeper can establish that the loss was due to the

---

246 *Minneapolis Fire and Marine Insurance Co v Matson Navigation Co* 352 P.2d 335

negligence of the guest him/herself. This can be illustrated by the case of *Shacklock v Ethorpe* itself.

The facts of the case were that the appellant (the plaintiff) had had jewellery stolen from her room at the Bull Hotel, Gerrard's Cross. On the day of the theft, the appellant went up to London in the morning. Before leaving the hotel, she had placed her jewels and money in a jewel-case which she locked. She then put the locked jewel-case in a crocodile leather dressing-case or dressing-bag with three locks, described by a police witness as 'fairly massive,' all of which she locked. Finally she placed the locked dressing-case under a luggage-stand in her bedroom on which there were some other articles of baggage. She did not lock her bedroom door or hand in the key at the office. When she returned in the evening, it was found that the dressing-case had been forced open and the jewel-case stolen. It was subsequently ascertained that the theft had been perpetrated by an expert thief, who had arrived at the hotel during her absence and taken an adjoining bedroom.

After stating the *prima facie* rule Lord Macmillan went on to establish that:

> "It has always been the law, however, that the innkeeper can escape liability if he can show that
>
> 'the negligence of the guest occasions the loss in such a way as that the loss would not have happened if the guest had used the ordinary care that a prudent man may be reasonably expected to have taken under the circumstances.'"[247]

In this case the defendant contended that the plaintiff had been negligent by leaving the jewellery in an unlocked room and by not depositing it with the hotel for safekeeping. On the first issue Lord Macmillan quoted with approval from the judgment of Montague Smith J in *Oppenheim v White Lion Hotel Co:*[248]

> "I agree that there is no obligation on a guest at an inn to

---

247 *Quoting from Erle J, in Cashill v Wright (1856) 6 E & B 891, at p 900.*
248 *(1871) LR 6 CP 515.*

lock his bedroom door. Though it is a precaution which a prudent man would take, I am far from saying that the omission to do so alone would relieve the innkeeper from his ordinary responsibility. The law of *Calye's case* may remain untouched. But the fact of the guest having the means of securing himself, and choosing not to use them is one which with the other circumstances of the case should be left to the jury. The weight of it must, of course, depend upon the state of society at the time and place. What would be prudent in a small hotel, in a small town, might be the extreme of imprudence at a large hotel in a city like Bristol, where probably 300 bedrooms are occupied by people of all sorts."

In this case the Bull Hotel was a small hotel with some 20 bedrooms, and was situated in a small country town. The internal arrangements were such that the comings and goings of guests and visitors were under the observation of the staff. The appellant had stayed there on several occasions, and knew how the hotel operated. It was not the practice of guests to lock their bedroom doors and leave their keys at the office. No notice requesting this to be done was placed in the bedrooms or anywhere else in the hotel. There were no duplicate keys or master key for the use of the staff, and on one occasion when the appellant had locked her bedroom door and taken the key away with her she found on her return that her bedroom had not been attended to, as the chambermaid could not get access to it. On that basis it was held that in respect of not locking her door the plaintiff had not been negligent.

As for not depositing her valuables with the hotel she was also found not negligent. The jewels themselves were not particularly valuable, 23 miscellaneous items varying in value from £120 to 10s, and, probably more significantly, she had been given the impression by staff at the hotel that the hotel did not have a safe.

In the *Oppenheim* case referred to by Lord Macmillan the facts were that the plaintiff, a traveller, had gone to an hotel at Bristol, arriving at

11pm. In the commercial room he took from his pocket a canvas bag containing £22 in gold, some silver, and a £5 note, and took out 6d to pay for some stamps. He was then shown to a bedroom on an upper storey, the door of which had a lock and a bolt, and the window of which looked out on to a balcony. He was informed by the chambermaid that the window was open, but nothing was said about locking the door. On going to bed he closed the door, but did not lock or bolt it, and placed his clothes, the bag of money being in one of the pockets, on a chair at his bed side. During the night someone entered his room by the door while he slept, and stole the bag and money.

The judge at first instance had directed the jury that the question for their consideration was whether the loss would or would not have happened if the plaintiff had used the ordinary care that a prudent man might reasonably be expected to have taken under the circumstances. Following that direction the jury had found the defendants not liable. On appeal this direction was approved and the jury verdict confirmed.

Property of others

The strict liability extends not only to the property of the guest brought to the hotel but also, as illustrated by the case of *Robins & Co v Gray*,[249] to the property of others so long as the property was received by the hotelkeeper as the luggage of the guest. The facts of the case were that a commercial traveller employed by a firm who dealt in sewing-machines went to stay at an inn, and whilst there machines were sent to him by his employers in the ordinary course of business for the purpose of selling them to customers in the neighbourhood. Before the goods were sent the innkeeper had been given express notice that they were the property of the guest's employers. The issue in the case was whether the hotel had a lien over the goods because the commercial traveller had left without paying his bill. In deciding this issue the Court of Appeal were firmly of the opinion that the existence of a lien was simply the other side of the coin of the hotelkeeper's strict liability for the guest's goods. If the hotelkeeper was under a strict

---

249 *[1895] 2 QB 501*

liability for the safekeeping of the goods he would have a lien over the goods and vice versa. In the words of Lord Esher MR:

> " ... the innkeeper's liability is not that of a bailee or pledgee of goods; he is bound to keep them safely. It signifies not, so far as that obligation is concerned, if they are stolen by burglars, or by the servants of the inn, or by another guest; he is liable for not keeping them safely unless they are lost by the fault of the traveller himself. That is a tremendous liability: it is a liability fixed upon the innkeeper by the fact that he has taken the goods in; and by law he has a lien upon them for the expense of keeping them as well as for the cost of the food and entertainment of the traveller."

On the facts the court held that the property had been received by the hotel as the luggage of the guest and therefore the hotel had a lien. By the same token the hotel would have been liable if the property had been lost or stolen. In the course of the decision the court was at pains to point out that in the circumstances the hotelkeeper was under a duty to receive not only the guest but his property as well and it could not discriminate between the traveller and his luggage:

> " ... the custom of the realm is that, unless there is some reason to the contrary in the exceptional character of the things brought, he must take in the traveller and his goods. He has not to inquire whether the goods are the property of the person who brings them or of some other person. If he does so inquire, the traveller may refuse to tell him, and may say, "What business is that of yours? I bring the goods here as my luggage, and I insist upon your taking them in"; or he may say, "They are not my property, but I bring them here as my luggage, and I insist upon your taking them in"; and then the innkeeper is bound by law to take them in."

Exclusion of Liability

It is important to note that not only is the burden of proof upon the hotelkeeper to prove the negligence of the guest but that liability cannot be excluded. According to the Law Reform Committee:

> "As the liability is based on the custom of the realm and not on contract, the innkeeper cannot escape liability by warning his guests to take special precautions, nor can he by any express contract restrict his liability."[250]

This was accepted in the case of *Williams v Linnit*[251] where a guest had his car stolen from the hotel car park. As we saw in Chapter One one of the issues in *Williams v Linnit* was whether the car had been parked within the *hospitium* or curtilage of the hotel. If so then the hotelkeeper was liable for its theft. If not then the hotelkeeper would only be liable if negligent in which case a notice could relieve him of liability. There was such a notice in the car park which stated:

> "Car Park. Patrons only. Vehicles are admitted to this parking place on condition that the proprietor shall not be liable for loss of or damage to (a) any vehicle (b) anything in or on or about any vehicle, however, such loss or damage may be caused. R. W. Linnitt. Proprietor."

In the court of first instance the judge had found that the plaintiff had not seen, or, at any rate, read, the notice and that, in any event, if the car park was part of the inn, such a notice would not relieve the innkeeper of his common law liability. The defendant, on appeal, did not seek to rely on this notice as contractually relieving him from liability, and conceded that, if the car park was within the *hospitium*, he could not contract out of his liability. On this issue Denning LJ dissented but the majority were of the opinion that the notice would

---

250 *Law Reform Committee Second Report, Innkeepers' Liability for Property of Travellers, Guests and Residents, Cmd 9161, 1954, para. 6.*

251 *[1951] 1 All ER 278*

not protect the hotelkeeper once it had been decided that the car park lay within the *hospitium* of the inn.[252]

Damage to Property

According to the Law Reform Committee[253] there was some doubt about whether the strict liability of the hotelkeeper extended to damage to property as opposed to loss or theft. *Winkworth v Raven,*[254] a case where a guest's car had been damaged by frost while standing in an unheated garage which was open on one side, held that the liability did not extend to damage as opposed to loss. However the Committee felt that the decision went further than necessary and could have been decided on narrower grounds – that the hotelkeeper's liability is satisfied by providing accommodation which is reasonably fit for its purpose. It was their view that liability did extend to damage as well as loss but they took the precaution of making a recommendation to that effect:

> "An innkeeper's liability in respect of damage to property should be the same as his liability for loss of the property."[255]

This recommendation was taken up by Parliament in section 1(2) of the Hotel Proprietors Act 1956:

> 1(2) The proprietor of an hotel shall, as an innkeeper, be under the like liability, if any, to make good to any guest of his any damage to property brought to the hotel as he would be under to make good the loss thereof.

---

252 *Note however that the Hotel Proprietors' Act 1956 has had the effect of overruling this case as far as liability for guests' cars is concerned.*

253 *Para. 8.*

254 *[1931] 1 KB 652. The case was followed by Williams v Owen [1956] 1 All ER 104.*

255 *Para. 16.*

Is the claimant a guest?

For a guest to take advantage of the protection afforded to his property he must of course establish that he is a guest. This issue arose in the case of *Strauss v The County Hotel and Wine Company Ltd.*[256] The facts of the case were that the plaintiff arrived at Carlisle with the intention of spending the night at the defendants' hotel, which adjoined the railway station. He delivered his luggage to one of the porters of the hotel, but, after reading a telegram which was waiting for him, decided not to spend the night at Carlisle, and went into the coffee-room to order some refreshments. He was not able to obtain in the coffee-room exactly what he required, and went into the station refreshment-room, which was under the same management as the hotel, and connected to it by a covered passage. Shortly afterwards he went out, telling the porter to lock up his luggage, and it was locked up in a room near the refreshment-room. On his return he found that part of it was missing. It was held that on the facts the plaintiff was not a guest at the time his luggage was stolen and therefore the hotelkeeper was not strictly liable for the luggage. According to Mathew J:

> "The counsel for the plaintiff were called upon to shew at what point of time the relation of landlord and guest commenced. They suggested that it was when the plaintiff gave his luggage to the porter. But at that time the plaintiff had not made up his mind to become a guest. The fact that he ordered his goods to be locked up, and that they were locked up, is no more than if he had said that he was uncertain whether he should stay in the inn, and that in the meantime he wished his goods to be locked up. In such a case there could be no liability."

Other exceptions to liability

At the outset it was said that the strict liability was subject to exceptions, the principal one being where the hotelkeeper could establish that the loss was due the negligence of the guest. For the sake

---

256 *(1883) 12 QBD 27*

of completeness it is necessary to mention that the other two exceptions are where the loss is due to Act of God or the actions of the Queen's enemies. There is also the case of *Farnworth v Packwood*[257] where the guest, by way of excessive caution, assumed the exclusive control of his room in such a way as to show an intention to relieve the hotelkeeper of liability.

Restrictions on Liability

Having examined the liability that an hotelkeeper has for the loss or damage of a guest's property we will now look at how the Hotel Proprietors Act (HPA) 1956 has limited the scope of the strict liability by restricting the definition of guest; by removing vehicles from the strict liability protection; and by permitting hotelkeepers to limit liability by means of suitably worded notices.

The Recommendations of the Law Reform Committee

In their Second Report[258] the Law Reform Committee were asked to consider whether any changes were desirable in the law relating to innkeepers' liability in respect of the property of travellers, guests and residents. In a brief but cogent report they made a number of recommendations which were enacted in the HPA 1956. We will look at these in turn. It is important to note however that the Committee's overall view was that strict liability should be maintained. Their recommendations did not fundamentally alter the strict liability basis for loss or damage to property. The rationale can be found in this passage:

> "9. It has been represented to us, notably by The Law Society, that the time has come for an alteration in the old common law liability of an innkeeper as an insurer of his guests' goods. The historical reasons for such a rule have, it is said, to a large extent disappeared. Travel is now very much more common than it used to be and travellers are

---

257 *(1816) Holt NP 209*
258 *Cmd. 9161, 1954*

no longer exposed to danger from highwaymen in league with innkeepers. There has, moreover, been a considerable growth in the number of residential hotels and similar places which are not inns, at which travellers do not have the benefit of the special protection afforded by the common law to those who stay at inns. For these reasons, it is suggested, innkeepers should be placed in the same position as the proprietors of residential hotels and similar establishments and their liability should depend upon negligence, thus removing an anomaly for which the justification is said to have disappeared.

10. We have given careful consideration to the views described in the last paragraph, more particularly as we think that there is considerable force in the argument that the distinction between inns and other places such as residential hotels which are not inns within the meaning of the law is not easy to defend in theory and, often at any rate, difficult to draw clearly in practice. We have come to the conclusion, however, that the principle of strict liability ought to be retained. Apart from the case of motor cars, to which we refer hereafter, the evidence which we have received shows few cases of hardship. That this is so is, we think, due to the universal practice of innkeepers in insuring against their liabilities. From enquiries which we have made, it would appear that in the case of the ordinary hotelkeeper's liability policy the proportion of the premium attributable to the strict liability of an innkeeper forms but a small proportion of the whole, and it is therefore unlikely, so far as his insurance premium is concerned, that an innkeeper would benefit to any appreciable extent by the abolition of the rule of strict liability. We think there is still good reason why persons who hold themselves out as being willing to provide food and lodging far all comers should be under a special obligation in regard to the safety of the goods which

travellers bring with them to the inn, and upon which in return the innkeeper, unlike the boarding house keeper, has a lien far his charges. (We should add that the evidence we have received satisfiés us that a substantial number of innkeepers attach considerable importance to the right to exercise, this lien.) And the fact that a new class of residential hotels and similar places has grown up does not seem to us to be a valid reason, for abolishing the old rule. The traveller is today as much as in the past exposed to the risk of loss, through neglect on the part of the innkeeper or his servants, but it is often by the nature of the case difficult, if not impossible, for him to prove negligence, as would be necessary in order to establish the innkeeper's liability if the law were to be altered in the manner suggested by The Law Society; unless, indeed, the burden of disproving negligence were placed on the innkeeper, an alteration which would not, we think, necessarily be acceptable to those who complain of the present law. We think it is not unreasonable that innkeepers should be expected to insure against liability far loss of travellers' goods on their premises. They can do so much more easily and very much more cheaply than the ordinary traveller could insure if the law were altered. We have in mind especially the personal belongings which such a traveller brings with him and which, unlike articles of jewellery, are rarely insured.

We are fortified in this conclusion by the similarity which exists between English law and the laws of many foreign countries under which special obligations are imposed upon innkeepers in regard to the safety of their guests' property. This applies not only to the countries which have accepted the common law, but also, we understand, to such countries as France, Germany and Switzerland."

The definition of guest

In Chapter One we saw that a 'guest' or 'traveller' has certain rights bestowed upon them by the law of innkeeping. One of these, currently under discussion, is the strict liability for their property. Guests at inns enjoyed the benefits of strict liability. Those who were not guests or who did not stay at an inn or hotel had to rely on the law of negligence. We also saw that the definition of guest had been extended over the years. Originally a guest was someone who stayed overnight but by the time the case of *Williams v Linnit* was decided in 1951[259] the definition encompassed anyone who stopped at the hotel for refreshment. The Committee pointed out that this caused an unsatisfactory distinction between someone who ate out at a restaurant and someone who took their meal at an inn. If the property of the former was lost or damaged he had to prove negligence whereas the latter was protected by strict liability. The Committee recommended that for the purposes of the protection of a guest's property the old concept of guest should be restored i.e. liability should only be strict in respect of the property of guests who stayed overnight. This recommendation was taken up by the government and can be found in the HPA 1956:

> 2(1) Without prejudice to any other liability incurred by him with respect to any property brought to the hotel, the proprietor of an hotel shall not be liable as an innkeeper to make good to any traveller any loss of or damage to such property except where–
>
> (a) at the time of the loss or damage sleeping accommodation at the hotel had been engaged for the traveller; and
>
> (b) the loss or damage occurred during the period commencing with the midnight immediately preceding, and ending with the midnight immediately following, a period for which the traveller was a guest at the hotel and entitled to use the accommodation so engaged.

---

259 *[1951] 1 KB 165*

Liability for vehicles

The Committee drew attention to the grievance expressed by the hotel industry at having to accept liability for the loss or damage of guests' motor vehicles – not only for those left overnight at the hotel but also, as in the case of *Williams v Linnit*, for cars parked while the owner had a meal. They felt that innkeepers suffered real hardship in such cases, more particularly because the car may have been parked without the knowledge of the innkeeper. They pointed out that as cars were almost invariably insured by their owners the question of liability was not an issue between the hotel and the guest but between two insurance companies. They recommended that liability in such cases should not be strict, but as a corollary, the innkeeper's lien should also be removed. This recommendation was also accepted by the government:

> 2(2) Without prejudice to any other liability or right of his with respect thereto, the proprietor of an hotel shall not as an innkeeper be liable to make good to any guest of his any loss of or damage to or have any lien on, any vehicle or any property left therein, or any horse or other live animal or its harness or other equipment.

Limitation of Liability

The Innkeepers Liability Act 1863 provided that in certain circumstances an innkeeper could limit his liability for guests' property to £30, subject to certain conditions being satisfied. The Committee felt that the Act had worked well but given the change in the value of money in the intervening period the sum should be raised to £100, although it should be confined to £50 for any one item. As a consequence of this recommendation the Innkeepers Liability Act 1863 was repealed and replaced by the following provisions:

> (3) Where the proprietor of an hotel is liable as an innkeeper to make good the loss of or any damage to property brought to the hotel, his liability to any one guest shall not exceed fifty pounds in respect of any

one article, or one hundred pounds in the aggregate, except where –

(a) the property was stolen, lost or damaged through the default, neglect or wilful act of the proprietor or some servant of his; or

(b) the property was deposited by or on behalf of the guest expressly for safe custody with the proprietor or some servant of his authorised, or appearing to be authorised, for the purpose, and, if so required by the proprietor or that servant, in a container fastened or sealed by the depositor; or

(c) at a time after the guest had arrived at the hotel, either the property in question was offered for deposit as aforesaid and the proprietor or his servant refused to receive it, or the guest or some other guest acting on his behalf wished so to offer the property in question but, through the default of the proprietor or a servant of his, was unable to do so:

Provided that the proprietor shall not be entitled to the protection of this subsection unless, at the time when the property in question was brought to the hotel, a copy of the notice set out in the Schedule to this Act printed in plain type was conspicuously displayed in a place where it could conveniently be read by his guests at or near the reception office or desk or, where there is no reception office or desk, at or near the main entrance to the hotel.

Apart from the increase in the limits of liability this substantially re-enacts the provisions of the 1863 Act. As we can see the limitations apply except in three circumstances

● The property was stolen, lost or damaged due to the fault of the hotelkeeper

● The property was deposited with the hotelkeeper for safekeeping

● A statutory notice was not displayed by the hotelkeeper.

The fault of the hotelkeeper

In *Belleville v Palatine*[260] the plaintiff had had her expensive fur coat stolen from her room while she was out. It was held that the hotel had exhibited the statutory notice prominently so unless she could prove that the theft was due to the fault of the hotelkeeper her damages would be limited to £30. She contended that the hotel was negligent in three respects. First, the key to Room 43, which the thief had been given, also fitted the lock to her room because the door had warped enabling the lock to be turned sufficiently for someone to enter. Second, the thief had arrived late at night with an apparently empty suitcase. Third, the chambermaid had discovered that two hand towels were missing from his room and he had hidden them under the cushion of the chair in the room. As far as the latter two factors are concerned the plaintiff felt that these were sufficient to put the hotel on notice and if they had been more vigilant the theft would not have occurred. The judge however felt that none of this amounted to negligence on the part of the defendant hotel and she was confined to £30 damages.

As with many such cases it turns on its specific facts and there is little of legal significance in it apart from a clear statement by the court that the burden of proof lay on the plaintiff to prove the default of the hotel.

Cryan v Hotel Rembrandt[261] is another case involving negligence. Here the plaintiff's coat was stolen after she had deposited it in a bedroom which was being used as a cloakroom. The judge held that this amounted to negligence:

> "In my judgment, to use as a cloak room a room which was intended for a bedroom, and one therefore which ought to be locked when the guest was not using it, without having somebody in charge, is negligence. Furthermore, it is usual

---

260 *171 LT 363*
261 *133 LT 395*

in the case of a cloakroom to deliver to the person depositing the coat etc, a ticket for the purpose of identifying the deposit, and this was not done. There was, therefore, negligence, not only within the statue but also at common law."

Deposited for safekeeping

In *Whitehouse v Picket*[262] the plaintiff had brought a bag of jewellery samples to the hotel with him. He had given the bag to the 'boots' of the hotel who had taken it to the hotel office, which also served as a bar, and put it in a recess. This had happened on previous occasions during the past 18 years. Later it was discovered that the bag had been stolen. Under the 1863 Act the defendants could limit their liability unless the goods had been 'expressly' deposited with them for safe keeping. In the opinion of Lord Loreburn this had not been done and the plaintiff was only entitled to the statutory sum:

"The word 'expressly' is not used without a purpose. It means that an intention by the bailor is not enough. That intention must be brought to the mind of the bailee or his agent in some reasonable and intelligible manner, so that he may, if so minded, insist on the precautions specified in the Act. The pursuer's traveller caused to be placed in the office, without a word spoken, a bag of undeclared contents, which was laid in a corner of the room; and there is nothing more of substance proved in this case on this point except that he had been in the habit of depositing similar property in that or an adjoining room for some years, also without word spoken. The Act meant to secure for the innkeeper, by warning, an opportunity of safeguarding himself when a heavy risk is place on him. There is no ground for saying he had such a warning here."

O'Connor v Grand International Hotel Co[263] is another case involving

---

262 *[1908] AC 357*
263 *[1898] 2 IR 92*

jewellery. In this case the plaintiff had handed a box of jewellery to the manageress of the hotel saying, "Keep that for me, I shall probably want it to-morrow." No indication of its value was communicated to the manageress. The court was of the unanimous opinion that the words he had used were not sufficient to amount to a deposit for safekeeping *under the Act*. The transaction was too casual to bring home to the defendant's employee that this was such a deposit. If more formal words had been used then the hotelkeeper would have been in a position to take the appropriate precautions.

Cryan v Rembrandt also turned on the issue of whether the coat was deposited for safekeeping but on the facts of the case the court held that placing them in the cloakroom/bedroom was sufficient evidence of this.

Statutory notice

The schedule to the 1956 Act contains the wording of the statutory notice:

> Loss of or Damage to Guests' Property
>
> Under the Hotel Proprietors Act 1956 a hotel proprietor may in certain circumstances be liable to make good any loss of or damage to a guest's property even though it was not due to any fault of the proprietor or staff of the hotel.
>
> This liability however–
>
> (a) extends only to the property of guests who have engaged sleeping accommodation at the hotel;
>
> (b) is limited to £50 for any one article and a total of £100 in the case of any one guest, except in the case of property which has been deposited, or offered for deposit, for safe custody;
>
> (c) does not cover motor-cars or other vehicles of any kind or any property left in them, or horses or other live animals.

> This notice does not constitute an admission either that the
> Act applies to this hotel or that liability thereunder attaches
> to the proprietor of this hotel in any particular case.

It is in much the same form as the statutory notice in the 1863 Act.
Failure to comply with it has serious consequences. In *Spice v Bacon*[264]
a seemingly minor omission left the hotelkeeper deprived of its
protection. An unintentional misprint resulted in the notice saying ' ...
stolen, lost, or injured, through the wilful default or neglect of such
innkeeper ...' instead of ' ... stolen, lost, or injured, through the wilful
act, default or neglect of such innkeeper ...' The court regarded this as
a material omission and the notice therefore did not comply with the
Act and was therefore ineffective.

In *Hodgson v Ford*[265] the hotelkeeper lost the benefit of the statutory
limitation because a notice had not been displayed, according to the
1863 Act in a 'conspicuous part of the hall or entrance to his inn'. In
Carey v Longs Hotel[266] there was a notice but it was placed on the first
floor rather than the entrance hall and this was not regarded as
compliance with the Act.

The 1956 Act is worded slightly differently. It requires the notice to be

> " ... conspicuously displayed in a place where it could
> conveniently be read by his guests at or near the reception
> office or desk or, where there is no reception office or
> desk, at or near the main entrance to the hotel"

Despite the obvious advantages of such a notice, which presumably
would be required by insurance companies, it is still quite common to
find hotels who do not display it, or if they do, it is not where it could
be 'conveniently' read, often placed on the wall at the back of
reception in a typeface which cannot be read at that distance.

---

264 *(1877) 2 ExD 463*
265 *(1892) 8 TLR 722*
266 *(1891) 7 TLR 213*

CHAPTER SEVEN
THE HOTELKEEPER'S LIEN

In the previous chapter we looked at the strict liability that the hotelkeeper has for guests' property in the event of loss or damage of that property. This article examines the corollary to this – that the innkeeper has a lien on the property of the guest in the event of the guest not paying for his accommodation and food. The justification for this is that as the innkeeper is under an obligation to receive both guests and their property then it is only fair to confer the right of lien on them to satisfy any debt the guest may incur. As Parke B, in *Sunbolf v Alford*[267] put it:

> "There can be no doubt that the innkeeper has by law a lien upon the goods of his guest, and that is upon the ground that he is bound to receive him, and must have some means given him by which he may be enabled to work out payment of his debt."

The Law Reform Committee expressed much the same view in its report that lead to the Hotel Proprietors' Act 1956[268] (HPA):

> "We think there is still good reason why persons who hold themselves out as being willing to provide food and lodging far all comers should be under a special obligation in regard to the safety of the goods which travellers bring with them to the inn, and upon which in return the innkeeper, unlike the boarding house keeper, has a lien for his charges. (We should add that the evidence we have received satisfies us that a substantial number of innkeepers attach considerable importance to the right to exercise this lien.)" (Para. 10)

---

267 (1838) 3 M&W 253
268 Cmd. 9161, 1954

A number of issues arise in respect of the exercise of the lien and these will be examined in turn.

The scope of the lien

Which property can be detained?

It used to be the case that the power of lien extended to any property that the guest brought to the hotel with him, including in many of the early cases, his horse, and latterly, his car. However this was changed by the HPA 1956 and vehicles and horses were excluded from the exercise of the hotelkeeper's lien.

> 2(2) Without prejudice to any other liability or right of his with respect thereto, the proprietor of an hotel shall not as an innkeeper ... have any lien on, any vehicle or any property left therein, or any horse or other live animal or its harness or other equipment.

The rationale for this was also explained in the Report of the Law Reform Committee:

> "There is in our view a substantial distinction between the car which a traveller brings with him to an inn and which unknown to the innkeeper, and contrary, perhaps, to his express instructions, the traveller may leave in a car park, and other property which the traveller takes inside the inn and over which the innkeeper accordingly has some measure of control. There is, moreover, the further point that it is common for owners of motor cars to insure against loss, so that frequently in the case of a claim against an innkeeper the contest is merely one between two insurance companies. We think therefore that it is reasonable that an innkeeper should no longer be under a strict liability in regard to motor vehicles (in which expression we should include motor bicycles) brought to the inn, with the corollary that he should no longer have a lien on them for his charges." (Para. 12)(Emphasis added)

The property of third parties

More controversial however is whether the lien extends to the property of third parties which the guest brings to the hotel. For instance in the case of *Threlfall v Borwick*[269] the guest stayed at the defendant's hotel in Windermere where he also had the use of a private sitting room. In the sitting room he placed a piano which he had brought with him. He left the hotel owing £45 to the hotelkeeper who exercised his right of lien over the piano in respect of this outstanding amount. It transpired that the piano belonged not to the guest but to the plaintiff, from whom it had been hired. It was held by the Court of Exchequer Chamber that the lien had been lawfully exercised over the piano even though it belonged to a third party. Lord Coleridge CJ said:

> "The plaintiff's counsel has said all that could be urged in support of his case, which is really hopeless. It is admitted that in general an innkeeper has a lien on all goods which the guest brings with him as his own, whether they are his own or another's; and the only question raised is, whether the lien extends to goods which the innkeeper would not have been bound to receive. I may say that I should be inclined to agree, if a guest brought a piano with him for his own amusement, that, according to the advanced usages of society, the innkeeper might be well held to be bound to receive it, if he has room for it. But it is quite unnecessary to decide that question, because we are all clearly of opinion that, the defendant having taken in the piano and safely kept it, it is too clear to be doubted that he has a lien upon it. Both on principle and authority the judgment must be affirmed."

This case however needs to be distinguished from an earlier case, *Broadwood v Granara*[270], also, strangely enough, involving a piano. In that case the guest, a professional musician, had stayed at the

---

269 *(1875) LR QB 210*
270 *(1854) 10 Ex 417*

defendant's hotel, the Hotel L'Europe in Leicester Square, and had had a piano delivered to him for his use, by the plaintiff. The guest ran up a large bill and the hotelkeeper exercised a lien over the piano. It was held that there was no right to exercise a lien over the piano. According to Pollock CB:

> "This is the case of goods, not brought to the inn by a traveller as his goods, either upon his coming to or whilst staying at the inn, but they are goods furnished for his temporary use by a third person, and known by the innkeeper to belong to that person. I shall not inquire, whether, if the pianoforte had belonged to the guest, the defendant would have had a lien on it. It is not necessary to decide that point, for the case finds that it was known to the defendant that the pianoforte was not the property of the guest, and that it was sent to him for a special purpose. Under those circumstances I am clearly of opinion that the defendant has no lien."

A further reason was given by Parke B:

> " ... inasmuch as the effect of such a lien is to give him a right to keep the goods of one person for the debt of another, the lien cannot be claimed except in respect of goods which, in performance of his duty to the public, he is bound to receive. The obligation to receive depends on his public profession. If he has only a stable for a horse he is not bound to receive a carriage. There was no ground whatever for saying that the defendant was under an obligation to receive this pianoforte."

The issue was further explored in the Court of Appeal case, *Robins v Gray*.[271] The facts of the case were that a commercial traveller employed by a firm who dealt in sewing-machines went to stay at an hotel, and whilst there machines were sent to him by his employers in the ordinary course of business for the purpose of selling them to

---

271 *[1895] 2 QB 501*

customers in the neighbourhood. Before the goods were sent the hotelkeeper had express notice that they were the property of the employers, but he received them as the baggage of the traveller, who subsequently left the inn without paying his bill for board and lodging. It was held that the lien had been properly exercised. *Broadwood v Granara* was referred to in all three judgments. All three of the judges were of the opinion that as the piano was not received by the hotelkeeper *as the guest's luggage or baggage* then no lien attached to it. In this case as the sewing machines were received as the baggage of the guest the hotelkeeper had a valid lien on them. Lord Esher MR gave a particularly trenchant view of the law on this issue:

> "I have no doubt about this case. I protest against being asked, upon some new discovery as to the law of innkeeper's lien, to disturb a well-known and very large business carried on in this country for centuries. The duties, liabilities, and rights of innkeepers with respect to goods brought to inns by guests are founded, not upon bailment, or pledge, or contract, but upon the custom of the realm with regard to innkeepers. Their rights and liabilities are dependent upon that, and that alone; they do not come under any other head of law. What is the liability of an innkeeper in this respect? If a traveller comes to an inn with goods which are his luggage – I do not say his personal luggage, but his luggage – the innkeeper by the law of the land is bound to take him and his luggage in. The innkeeper cannot discriminate and say that he will take in the traveller but not his luggage. If the traveller brought something exceptional which is not luggage – such as a tiger or a package of dynamite – the innkeeper might refuse to take it in; but the custom of the realm is that, unless there is some reason to the contrary in the exceptional character of the things brought, he must take in the traveller and his goods.
>
> ...

> I am of opinion that an innkeeper is bound to take in goods with which a person who comes to the inn is travelling as his goods, unless they are of an exceptional character; that the innkeeper's lien attaches, and that the question of whose property the goods are, or of the innkeeper's knowledge as to whose property they are, is immaterial, This appeal should, therefore, be dismissed."

And AL Smith LJ addressed the issue of the knowledge of the hotelkeeper as to the ownership of the goods by a third party:

> "Some expressions of judges were relied on to the effect that an innkeeper had a lien upon goods brought to his inn by a guest, if the innkeeper did not know that the goods were not the property of the guest, but were the property of some one else. There is no decision, however, that if he did know his lien was gone. The illustration may be put of goods received by an innkeeper of which one-half belonged to the guest who brought them, and the other half to some one else. Suppose the innkeeper received all the goods with knowledge of the fact: could it be said that he was under any different obligation with respect to the goods which were the guest's and those which were not; so that, as to one half, his obligation was to keep the goods safely and securely, and, as to the other, only to take due care? In my judgment, the contention made on behalf of the appellants fails, and I agree that this appeal should be dismissed."

Thus the law seems quite straightforward. The lien attaches to any goods the guest brings to the hotel with him so long as they are received by the hotelkeeper as the guest's luggage, whether or not the goods belong to a third party and whether or not the hotelkeeper knew that.

In what capacity were the goods received?

Even if goods have been received by the hotelkeeper they must have been received as the luggage of the guest. This point was in issue in the case of *Berman & Nathans Ltd v Weibye.*[272] The defendants were hotelkeepers who had received guests whose accommodation was paid for by a film company. The film company also arranged for costumes, owned by the plaintiffs, to be stored at the hotel. When the guests left, the bill for their accommodation and board had not been fully paid. The defendants sought to exercise a lien over the costumes owned by the plaintiffs. After explaining that the law of Scotland was the same as the law for England in cases such as this i.e. a lien exists over a guest's property even though it is the property of a third party Lord Emslie nevertheless decided that there was no lien over the costumes as they had not been received by the hotel as the luggage of the guests.

> "The relevancy of the defender's averments requires only to be tested by asking whether the costumes delivered into the defender's keeping by Panda [the film company] in this case could reasonably be held to be ... "possessions" of the named individuals, the bills in respect of whose accommodation in the hotel remained unpaid by Panda. The answer to that question is not in doubt. If these costumes had been damaged while they were in store in the defender's hotel no members of "the party," the composition of which changed from time to time, would have had, singly or collectively, any title to sue the defender ... Mr Stein [counsel for the defendants] very properly conceded that this was so and if I may say so it was a concession which could not reasonably have been withheld. As Mr Stein also very properly accepted, the loss in the circumstances figured would have been Panda's loss alone. The costumes at no time came to be included, or identified as being, within the possessions of any of the individuals who stayed in the hotel, singly or as a group ... They were delivered by Panda. They were accepted by the defender from Panda. The obligation to pay the charges made by the defender in relation to the costumes rested upon Panda alone."

---

272 *1983 SLT 299*

Stolen goods

But what if the goods have been stolen? Does the lien attach to stolen goods? *Marsh v Commissioner of Police & McGee*[273] is a case in point. The facts of the case were that a guest had stayed at the Ritz Hotel in London and on being asked to pay had offered a ring as security. He then left the hotel without paying his bill and it later transpired that the ring had been stolen from the plaintiffs. One of the issues in dispute was whether or not the hotel had a lien on the stolen property of a third party. Lord Goddard was unequivocally of the opinion that there would be a lien:

> "It has not been contested – and the authorities seem to be perfectly clear and uniform on the point – that an innkeeper's lien will attach to property brought by a guest to the hotel although the property has been stolen. I need not refer to all the cases which have been cited, but *Gordon v Silber*[274] is a clear authority on that point, and the law was also stated thus in *Robins & Co v Gray*"

There was another issue raised in the case which was whether the ring had been given as security in a completely separate transaction, but this was dismissed by Du Parcq LJ on the basis that the evidence was not sufficient to support such a finding. Lord Goddard was more robust in his treatment of this point:

> "I want to say one thing about the view which was taken by the Divisional Court. Lord Caldecote C.J. said:
>
> > 'On the facts of the present case it is, I think, clear that the hotel proprietors did not exercise an innkeeper's lien on this ring for the simple reason that they were never in a position to do so until the time came when the guest, owing a bill which he was unable to pay, produced and handed the ring to the innkeeper as security for the payment of the debt.'

273 *[1944] 2 All ER 392*
274 *(1890) 25 QBD 491*

The Lord Chief Justice, apparently, considered the handing over of the ring as an entirely separate and independent transaction amounting to a pledge. With all respect I am unable to agree. The lien attaches to property, contained in luggage, although the innkeeper does not know what goods are contained in the luggage, and it attaches although the occasion for exercising it does not arise until the guest has incurred a debt, and has been presented with a bill, and seeks to leave the hotel without paying the bill. It seems clear in this case, that the justices could find that this ring was brought into the hotel by the guest in his capacity and character as a guest, and, therefore, whether the innkeepers knew it was there or not, does not matter. The lien attached to it and, as soon as the innkeepers knew of the existence of the ring, they could exercise their lien on it. It makes no difference in law whether the guest produced the ring and said: 'There you are. I owe you a debt and you can exercise your lien on this'; or whether the innkeeper laid his hand on it and said: 'I am going to exercise my lien on this.'"

Marsh can be distinguished from the case of *Matsuda v Waldorf Hotel Company Limited*[275] In that case the guest at the hotel borrowed money from the defendant hotelkeeper on the security of three railway tickets that had been stolen from the plaintiff. It was held that moneylending was no part of the business of an innkeeper and that no question of an innkeeper's lien arose. The tickets had been acquired as a result of a separate bargain altogether and the plaintiff was entitled to possession of them.

Damage to the hotel

Even if there is a *prima facie* case for the exercise of the lien there is still a question of what debts it can be exercised in respect of. This was an issue which arose in the Scottish case of *Ferguson v Peterkin*.[276]

---

275 *(1910) 27 TLR 153*
276 *1953 SLT (Sh Ct) 91*

The facts of the case were that the plaintiffs were guests at the defendant's hotel in Edinburgh. While they were there a door fell off the wardrobe in their room. When the guests checked out the hotelkeeper wished to charge them for both their room and board and for the damage to the wardrobe. When the guests refused to pay for the damaged wardrobe the hotelkeeper retained their luggage – including not only their clothes but also their passports (they were visitors from South Africa), ration books, pension book and cheque book. The property was returned after 48 days but in the meantime this caused them some considerable inconvenience. In entering judgment for the plaintiffs the judge held that the lien extended only to the amount owed for bed and board. It was not a general lien covering any debts unconnected with the contract for bed and board:

> "An hotel-keeper has a lien or right of retention over the luggage of his guest for the amount of his bill. In my opinion, this extends only to the account for the board and entertainment of the guest, while staying at the hotel. Whether it be based on implied obligation in a particular mutual contract and operates as a security for performance of the counterpart or depends on custom, it is a special lien. It is not a general lien in the sense that it provides a right in security covering debts or claims unconnected with the original contract."

As for the damage to the wardrobe the judge held that this was not a case of *res ipsa loquitur*. It was for the hotel to prove negligence on the part of the guests and this they had failed to do.

Detention of the guest

What lengths can the hotelkeeper go to to exercise his lien? This question was addressed in the case of *Sunbolf v Alford* mentioned above. The facts of the case were that the plaintiff and his friends had visited the defendant's inn and run up a bill of 11s 3d. On leaving they refused to pay the bill – for reasons which are not revealed in the report of the case. The defendant then stripped the coat from the back of the plaintiff in order to take it as security for the payment of the bill.

The plaintiff sued the innkeeper for assault and battery. The case turned on whether the defendant had a lien over the plaintiff's coat.

Lord Abinger CB discussed first whether the innkeeper could detain the person of the guest in order to exercise the lien. He found it difficult to restrain his indignation on this point:

> "If an innkeeper has the right to detain the person of his guest for the non-payment of his bill, he has a right to detain him until the bill is paid, – which may be for life; so that this defence supposes, that, by the common law, a man who owes a small debt, for which he could not be imprisoned by legal process, may yet be detained by an innkeeper for life. The proposition is monstrous. Again, if he have any right to detain the person, surely he is a judge in his own cause; for, he is then the party to determine whether the amount of his bill is reasonable, and he must detain him till the man brings an action against him for false imprisonment, and then if it were determined that the charge was not reasonable, and it appeared that the party had made an offer of a reasonable sum, the detainer would be unlawful. But, where is the law that say a man shall detain another for his debt without process of law?"

He went on to discuss the issue of whether the clothes could be taken from the back of the plaintiff:

> "As to a lien upon the goods, there are undoubtedly cases of exception to the general law in favour of particular claims; and if any innkeeper has the possession of the goods, and his debt is not paid, he has a right to detain them by virtue of that possession: but I do not agree that the has any right to take a parcel or other property out of the possession of the guest ... It appear to me, therefore, ... that the plea is in principle utterly bad, and that there is no ground for the attempt to justify an assault, under the pretence of detaining a man for a debt due to an innkeeper. It is also bad under the pretence of justifying the stripping

the plaintiff's coat off his back, and thereby inviting a breach of the peace, and making an assault necessary in order to exercise the right to the lien on the coat. It has been said justly, that in the case of a distress, where the taking of goods as a pledge for the debt is allowed, – the law is in favour of personal liberty, and where goods are in the actual possession and use of the debtor, they cannot be distrained. A man's clothes cannot be taken off his back in execution of a *fieri facias*."

Parke B provided another justification for the lien not extending to the plaintiff's clothes:

"But there is, at all events, no power to do what this plea justifies – namely, to strip the guest of his clothes; for, if there be, then, if the innkeeper take the coat off his back, and that prove to be an insufficient pledge, he may go on and strip him naked; and that would apply either to a male or to a female. That is a consequence so utterly absurd, that it cannot be entertained for a moment. Wearing apparel on a man's person (even if it does not extend to goods in the possession of the person) cannot be taken under a *fieri facias* or under an extent."

These two extracts leave no doubt that the hotelkeeper cannot detain the guest himself nor can he take the clothes from the guest's back but there remains a small doubt as to whether the guest's luggage can be taken from the guest's possession. Lord Abinger seemed to think not:

"I do not agree that the has any right to take a parcel or other property out of the possession of the guest"

However Parke B left the door open a little:

"Wearing apparel on a man's person (*even if it does not extend to goods in the possession of the person*) cannot be taken ... " [Emphasis added]

Of these two dicta the former seems the preferable position. If the justification for not permitting the clothes to be stripped from the guest's back is that it would amount to an assault and a breach of the peace then it is only a small step to take to say that the same justification can apply to wresting the luggage from the guest's hand. One can imagine the mayhem that could result at the reception desk if the guest resisted the hotelkeeper's attempts to exercise his lien. (See [2007] ITLJ 44 for an account of such an incident.)

Powers of Sale

Assuming that the hotelkeeper has exercised his lien successfully how can he recoup his losses? It used to be the case that all the hotelkeeper could do was to retain the luggage until the guest decided to pay. There was no power to sell the luggage except in certain limited jurisdictions.[277] Now however there is a statutory power of sale contained in the Innkeepers Act 1878. Section One provides:

> The landlord, proprietor, keeper, or manager of any hotel inn or licensed public-house shall, in addition to his ordinary lien, have the right absolutely to sell and dispose by public auction of any goods chattels carriages horses wares or merchandise which may have been deposited with him or left in the house he keeps, or in the coach-house stable stable-yard or other premises appurtenant or belonging thereunto, where the person depositing or leaving such goods chattels carriages horses wares or merchandise shall be or become indebted to the said innkeeper either for any board or lodging or for the keep and expenses of any horse or other animals left with or standing at livery in the stables or fields occupied by such innkeeper.
>
> Provided, that no such sale shall be made until after the said goods chattels carriages horses wares or merchandise shall have been for the space of six weeks in such charge or

---

277 *In London and Exeter there was a special custom entitling the hotelkeeper to sell goods retained under a lien.*

custody or in or upon such premises without such debt having been paid or satisfied, and that such innkeeper, after having, out of the proceeds of such sale, paid himself the amount of any such debt, together with the costs and expenses of such sale, shall on demand pay to the person depositing or leaving any such goods chattels carriages horses wares or merchandise the surplus (if any) remaining after such sale: Provided further, that the debt for the payment of which a sale is made shall not be any other or greater debt than the debt for which the goods or other articles could have been retained by the innkeeper under his lien.

Provided also, that at least one month before any such sale the landlord, proprietor, keeper, or manager shall cause to be inserted in one London newspaper and one country newspaper circulating in the district where such goods chattels carriages horses wares or merchandise, or some of them, shall have been deposited or left, an advertisement containing notice of such intended sale, and giving shortly a description of the goods and chattels intended to be sold, together with the name of the owner or person who deposited or left the same where known.

The operation of the Act was discussed in *Chesham Automobile Supply Limited v Beresford Hotel Ltd.*[278] The facts of the case were that when a guest had left the defendant hotel he owed money for his accommodation and food and also a small amount for sums that had been lent to him by the hotel. He left behind him a car belonging to the plaintiffs which he had hired from them. After four weeks the hotel had sent the car to a firm of auctioneers but it had broken down and had had to be repaired at the expense of the hotel. Subsequently, after the requisite advertisements had been placed in London and local newspapers, and after a period of six weeks had elapsed, the defendants sold the car at auction. The case turned on whether or not

---

278 29 TLR 584

---

the hotel had lost its lien and also the amount that could be retained out of the sale price of the car to cover the debts incurred by the guest.

The plaintiffs contended that when the car had been sent to the auctioneers the hotel had lost its lien because by sending it to the auctioneers and the repairer it had not remained in the possession of the defendants. The judge dismissed this argument, saying that the car had been received by the auctioneers and the repairers as agents for the defendants ' ... in whose real charge it was for the purpose and within the meaning of the Act.'

Quoting from *Mulliner v Florence*[279] the judge said that the innkeeper

> "' ... must not dispose of the chattel so as to give some one else a right of possession as against himself'. If he does he loses his lien, but so long as he retains the charge of the chattel and can enforce delivery of it to the guest if necessary ... he retains his lien even though the chattel may be removed for an authorised purpose from the premises."

The judge also awarded the cost of repairs, the advertisements and of arranging the sale of the car. However he disallowed the sums lent to the guest as the lien did not cover these.

Credit Card Pre-Authorisation: An Alternative to the Lien?

What has emerged from the discussion above is how antiquated the hotelkeeper's lien appears to be, as emphasised by the case law, much of which is from the 19th Century or even earlier. And this is a trend which will surely continue, driven largely by the ubiquity of the credit card. It is almost universal now, when checking into an hotel, to be asked to 'pre-authorise' a credit card payment. In the event that the guest 'does a runner' without paying for the food or accommodation contracted for the hotelkeeper can debit the appropriate amount from the guest's credit card. From the hotelkeeper's perspective this is a much more satisfactory method of obtaining payment than detaining the guest's luggage and then having to dispose of it.

---

279 *(1878) 3 QBD 484*

The question arises however as to what the 'pre-authorisation' covers and therefore what amounts can be debited from the card holders account? Does it cover only the accommodation or does it cover restaurant meals as well, and also drink from the minibar and phone charges? And what about alleged damage to the guest's room as in *Ferguson v Peterkin* discussed above? Can the hotelkeeper make a charge for that as well?

Before discussing this it is perhaps useful to explain exactly what pre-authorisation means and what happens when it occurs. According to the Barclaycard Business Procedure Guide[280]

> "Pre-authorisation allows you [the hotel] to estimate the final bill and reserve those funds on the card number while the customer is with you."

What this means is that the hotel informs the credit card company that you will be incurring say £150 worth of expenditure and ascertains that that amount is available on your card. If it is, then the card issuer 'ring fences' that amount from your credit limit. (This is a fact that many people are not aware of and are sometimes embarrassed by if the sum is a large one and reduces the credit limit accordingly, meaning that when the card is presented to purchase other goods and services the cardholder may be refused because the credit limit has been exceeded.) Nothing however is debited from your account at that time. The next morning when you come to pay your bill you present your card again and the actual amount of the bill is debited from your account and you sign for it (or enter your pin number). The amount that has been pre-authorised is then ignored. (Although if you pay using another card the hotel has to cancel the pre-authorisation in a separate transaction.) If you do not pay your bill on leaving it is only then that the hotel 'activates' the pre-authorisation and debits the amount from your account. If the amount of your bill exceeds the pre-authorised amount then the hotel will have to obtain a further authorisation.

---

280 *http://www.epdq.com/existing_customers/procedures_guides/procedure_guide.pdf*

The problem is that often it is not spelt out in any detail exactly what the pre-authorisation covers. Often the 'agreement' is informal in the extreme. It is not uncommon for the staff at the reception desk merely to ask for an imprint of the card without specifying what amount has been pre-authorised or what it will cover. It is common practice with at least two leading hotel chains that for a room costing in the order of £100 per night to pre-authorise another £50 and the guest would not be told of this unless they asked. Sometimes they will indicate that it covers 'extras' such as the minibar and telephone charges. Sometimes the guest is told that no money will be debited from the guest's account, which is technically correct but somewhat misleading, and may cause the guest to wonder what the point of it is.

Contrast this situation with a similar situation, car hire, where credit card pre-authorisation is also the norm. Here the consumer will be presented with a formal written contract stating precisely what they might be liable for and what can be charged to their credit card – including damage to the vehicle which may not be the consumer's fault and traffic violations and parking charges. In such cases it would be hard for the consumer to argue that there was not at least a *prima facie* case for debiting their account.

This approach is contractual in nature. The car hire company is able to make certain debits from the credit card on the basis that this has been agreed by the hirer. Similarly, if the hotel is to be able to debit the guest's card then it must have some kind of agreement with the guest. Given the informal nature of the process it might be difficult for the hotel to establish exactly what the terms of the agreement are. If we apply the 'officious bystander' test it would probably be fairly straightforward to establish that the purpose of the transaction was to cover those items that the guest would have expected to pay for if asked for cash i.e. accommodation and food purchased from the hotel. But what if those sums were disputed or other sums were added to the bill which the guest had not agreed to e.g. the damage to the wardrobe as in *Ferguson v Peterkin*, car parking, 'resort fees', service charges etc? It might be difficult for the hotel to prove that these were agreed by the guest and therefore any pre-authorisation might not cover this. No case law exists on the subject so any dispute would largely be determined on common law principles – contract and misrepresentation – with the guest being able to invoke such consumer protection legislation as the Unfair Contract Terms Act 1977 and the Unfair Terms in Consumer Contracts Regulations 1999.[281]

---

281 *SI 1999/2083*

APPENDIX ONE

HOTEL PROPRIETORS ACT 1956

1956 CHAPTER 62

Long Title

An Act to amend the law relating to inns and innkeepers

Enactment Clause

BE IT ENACTED by the Queen's most Excellent Majesty, by and with the advice and consent of the Lords Spiritual and Temporal, and Commons, in this present Parliament assembled, and by the authority of the same, as follows:–

1 Inns and innkeepers

(1) An hotel within the meaning of this Act shall, and any other establishment shall not, be deemed to be an inn; and the duties, liabilities and rights which immediately before the commencement of this Act by law attached to an innkeeper as such shall, subject to the provisions of this Act, attach to the proprietor of such an hotel and shall not attach to any other person.

(2) The proprietor of an hotel shall, as an innkeeper, be under the like liability, if any, to make good to any guest of his any damage to property brought to the hotel as he would be under to make good the loss thereof.

(3) In this Act, the expression "hotel" means an establishment held out by the proprietor as offering food, drink and, if so required, sleeping accommodation, without special contract, to any traveller presenting himself who appears able and willing to pay a reasonable sum for the services and facilities provided and who is in a fit state to be received.

2 Modifications of liabilities and rights of innkeepers as such

(1) Without prejudice to any other liability incurred by him with respect to any property brought to the hotel, the proprietor of an hotel shall not be liable as an innkeeper to make good to any traveller any loss of or damage to such property except where—

(a) at the time of the loss or damage sleeping accommodation at the hotel had been engaged for the traveller; and

(b) the loss or damage occurred during the period commencing with the midnight immediately preceding, and ending with the midnight immediately following, a period for which the traveller was guest at the hotel and entitled to use the accommodation so engaged.

(2) Without prejudice to any other liability or right of his with respect thereto, the proprietor of an hotel shall not as an innkeeper be liable to make good to any guest of his any loss of or damage to, or have any lien on, any vehicle or any property left therein, or any horse or other live animal or its harness or other equipment.

(3) Where the proprietor of an hotel is liable as an innkeeper to make good the loss of or any damage to property brought to the hotel, his liability to any one guest shall not exceed fifty pounds in respect of any one article, or one hundred pounds in the aggregate, except where—

(a) the property was stolen, lost or damaged through the default, neglect or wilful act of the proprietor or some servant of his; or

(b) the property was deposited by or on behalf of the guest expressly for safe custody with the proprietor or some servant of his authorised, or appearing to be authorised, for the purpose, and, if so required by the proprietor or that servant, in a container fastened or sealed by the depositor; or

(c) at a time after the guest had arrived at the hotel, either the property in question was offered for deposit as aforesaid and the proprietor or his servant refused to receive it, or the guest or some other guest acting on his behalf wished so to offer the property in question but, through the default of the proprietor or a servant of his, was unable to do so:

Provided that the proprietor shall not be entitled to the protection of this subsection unless, at the time when the property in question was brought to the hotel, a copy of the notice set out in the Schedule to this Act printed in plain type was conspicuously displayed in a place where it could conveniently be read by his guests at or near the reception office or desk or, where there is no reception office or desk, at or near the main entrance to the hotel.

3 Short title, repeal, extent and commencement

(1) This Act may be cited as the Hotel Proprietors Act 1956.

(2) ...

(3) This Act shall not extend to Northern Ireland.

(4) This Act shall come into operation on the first day of January, nineteen hundred and fifty-seven.

SCHEDULE NOTICE: LOSS OF OR DAMAGE TO GUESTS' PROPERTY

Section 2

Schedule Notice: Loss of or Damage to Guests' Property

Under the Hotel Proprietors Act 1956 a hotel proprietor may in certain circumstances be liable to make good any loss of or damage to a guest's property even though it was not due to any fault of the proprietor or staff of the hotel.

This liability however—

(a) extends only to the property of guests who have engaged sleeping accommodation at the hotel;

(b) is limited to £ 50 for any one article and a total of £ 100 in the case of any one guest, except in the case of property which has been deposited, or offered for deposit, for safe custody;

(c) does not cover motor-cars or other vehicles of any kind or any property left in them, or horses or other live animals.

This notice does not constitute an admission either that the Act applies to this hotel or that liability thereunder attaches to the proprietor of this hotel in any particular case.

INDEX

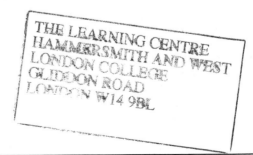